VIKING EXPANSION WESTWARDS

A BODLEY HEAD ARCHAEOLOGY

Viking Expansion Westwards

MAGNUS MAGNUSSON

Drawings by
ROSEMONDE NAIRAC

THE BODLEY HEAD · London Sydney Toronto

Tenth-century bronze
figurine of Thór from
Eyjafjörd in North
Iceland. Actual height,
three inches

© Magnus Magnusson 1973
Drawings © The Bodley Head Ltd 1973
ISBN 0 370 01577 0
Printed and bound in Great Britain for
The Bodley Head Ltd
9 Bow Street, London WC2E 7AL
by William Clowes & Sons Ltd, Beccles
Filmset in Monophoto Ehrhardt by
BAS Printers Ltd, Wallop, Hampshire
First published 1973

CONTENTS

AUTHOR'S NOTE

This book draws heavily on the work of a host of scholars, both past and present—far too many to mention individually in the text. Many of their names are to be found in the book-list for further reading on page 149; but in addition I owe thanks to many archaeologists and historians who have gone out of their way to give me help and advice on problems they have been studying. In particular I would like to mention Dr Breandán Ó Ríordáin of Dublin for showing me around the Viking city he is excavating there, and Dr Anna Ritchie of Edinburgh for much sound guidance on Viking antiquities in Scotland and for generously allowing me access to unpublished reports of her recent excavation at Buckquoy in the Orkneys. I am grateful, too, to the BBC and my colleagues on 'Chronicle' for the opportunity to visit many of the sites discussed in this book. But my major debt of gratitude is to Professor David M. Wilson of University College, London, who kindly read this book in manuscript and offered a number of helpful and illuminating suggestions.

INTRODUCTION

On the flat farmlands of Lower Gokstad, in Norway, there used to be a great mound, a large oblong hillock some 160 feet long and 16 feet high. It was not far from the village of Sandefjord, on the western side of Oslo Fjord, and lay about two miles from the sea. It had always been known locally as *Kongshaugen*—the King's Mound; and people in the district were convinced it was the burial mound of a king from ancient times and contained treasure.

Fired by dreams of buried wealth, the sons of the farmer at Lower Gokstad started digging into the mound early in January 1880. The ground was still frozen hard, and they made little headway, but they came across a great quantity of moss and hazel branches and wooden chips that had clearly been worked by human hands. News of what was going on at Lower Gokstad reached the ears of members of the Antiquarian Society in Oslo. Their president, Nicolay Nicolaysen, hurried the fifty miles from Oslo to put a stop to the work: the old stories might be true after all, and the great mound might conceal something of archaeological importance.

In April of that year Nicolaysen himself started excavating the mound. His plan was to drive an exploratory trench right through the base of the mound from south to north; and almost at once he struck lucky. On only the second day of digging he uncovered the wooden prow of a ship that was pointing directly towards the sea. He had found what has become the most famous Viking ship in the world—the Gokstad Ship.

It took Nicolaysen two and a half months to clear away all the soil that had been heaped on top of the ship to make the burial mound. At last the ship itself stood clear; the problem now was how to transport

it to Oslo. It was pulled from the demolished mound by winches, and then sawn into two halves amidships. Nine horses were used to draw the two halves on a wheeled sledge down the road to the seashore, where they were loaded onto a raft and pulled by steam tug across the fjord to Oslo. There the Gokstad Ship was carefully reconstituted and is now one of the major attractions of the Viking Ship Museum.

The ship had been used for a royal funeral late in the ninth century. It had been laid in a deep trench cut into the blue clay underlying the ground surface, and this clay had preserved the timber in almost perfect condition because it sealed the ship from any contact with the air. Only the upper parts of the stem and stern had rotted away where they had protruded above the bed of clay. The ship had seen much service, for it was about fifty years old when it was used for the funeral at Gokstad, but it would still have been seaworthy. Just aft of amidships, behind the mast, a large timber chamber had been built on a platform lying across the gunwales. On a bed inside lay the skeleton of a powerfully-built man of around fifty years of age, five feet ten inches tall. The condition of the bones showed that he had suffered severely from arthritis or gout. He had been buried surrounded by his weapons and accoutrements and personal possessions and accompanied by an odd menagerie of slaughtered animals—twelve horses, six dogs and a peacock. The dead man has been tentatively identified as King Olaf of Vestfold, who died near Gokstad around 890 AD.

The Gokstad Ship is one of the most beautiful vessels ever built. It was made chiefly of oak, and was about seventy-six feet long and seventeen feet broad. It weighed about twenty metric tons fully laden, and yet drew only about three feet. The mast carried a large square sail, a large steering paddle was mounted near the stern on the starboard side, and there were sixteen pairs of oars for manoeuvring in narrow waters or when the wind failed. The normal complement would have been no more than thirty-five men on long voyages. Long, lean, light and swift, it was perfect of its kind—a warship that could operate anywhere, in deep seas and shallow rivers alike. It was essentially a coastal vessel, but a replica of the ship that was made in 1893 proved its versatility by crossing the North Sea and the Atlantic from Norway to Newfoundland in stormy weather in twenty-eight days.

The Gokstad Ship was a typical Viking longship. In its time this was the most sophisticated vessel in the world, the outcome of centuries of technological innovation and development. It was the

Excavating the Gokstad Ship from a funeral mound in Norway in 1880.

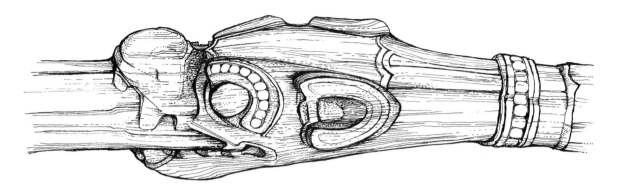

The carved tiller of
the Gokstad Ship

longship that made the Viking Age possible.

The term 'Viking Age' is in some respects an unfortunate one. The Vikings have always been portrayed as pirates, merciless barbarians who plundered and burned their way through Europe, heedless of their own lives and the lives of others, intent only on destruction and pillage. This deep-rooted popular prejudice about the Vikings can be traced back directly to the sensationalism of ecclesiastical writers who were the occasional victims of Viking raids. In a turbulent period, when piracy and casual raiding were a commonplace of everyday life all over Europe, the Vikings happened to be more successful at it than most other people; and they paid the price by getting an extremely bad reputation. The word Viking has come to mean anyone who came from Scandinavia in the Middle Ages, whether he was a farmer, a seaman, a merchant, a poet, an artist, a warrior, an explorer, a settler—or a raider. The term 'Viking Age' is used indiscriminately to cover three centuries of dynamic Scandinavian expansion that took place from around 800 AD onwards.

Yet in their time the Vikings were as much admired as feared and hated. Local chieftains all over Europe welcomed them as allies in their own political squabbles. In Scandinavian folklore they became the embodiment of hardy heroism and manly virtue. Nostalgic stories about the Vikings were the 'thrillers' of the day. And every boy dreamed of becoming a Viking himself one day:

> 'My mother once told me
> She'd buy me a longship,
> A handsome-oared vessel
> To go sailing with Vikings:
> To stand at the stern-post
> And steer a fine warship,

> Then head back for harbour,
> And hew down some foemen.'
> (From *Egil's Saga*)

Yet curiously enough, no one really knows what the word Viking actually means. It seems to be related to the Old Icelandic word *vík*, meaning 'bay' or 'creek'; so that a Viking possibly meant someone who lurked with his ship in a hidden bay. Other scholars think it derives from the old name for the land area around Oslo Fjord, the *Vík*, meaning someone who originally came from this southern part of Norway. Some think it may derive from the Old Icelandic verb *víkja*, meaning 'turn aside', so that a Viking was someone who made a detour or absented himself from home; while others look for a derivation in the Anglo-Saxon word *wic*, meaning 'military camp', so that a Viking was merely any armed warrior. There is a further complication, in that Old Icelandic has both the masculine noun *víkingur* (a Viking) and the feminine noun *víking* (meaning 'pirate raid'). A Viking, in effect, went on a viking—he went a-viking.

If the origin of the word Viking is obscure, so too is the cause of the Viking Age itself. There is no single, simple reason why the Scandinavians should suddenly have burst upon the European scene around 800 AD. Nor were the Vikings a single, homogeneous people, imbued with the same aims and ambitions. The three Scandinavian countries each had their distinct if sometimes overlapping spheres of influence—the Swedes in the Baltic and Russia, the Danes on the continent and in England, the Norwegians in Scotland and Ireland and the North Atlantic islands.

It was late in the eighth century that the Norwegians started spilling out of their homeland and moving west. It was not, however, a 'national' movement: Norway was not a nation at this time. It consisted of a scatter of inhabited areas along the long western seaboard, with a concentration of population in the south-west. Even the name Norway (*Norvegur*) simply meant 'North Way'—not so much a nation as a trade-route.

It is not yet clear why this emigration from Norway should have taken place, but archaeology and the study of place-names help to answer the question. It seems that early in the seventh century there was an increase of population that led to some movement up into the mountain valleys and forests where no one had tried to make a livelihood before. This population explosion and the consequent need for more land could be one explanation for widespread emigration.

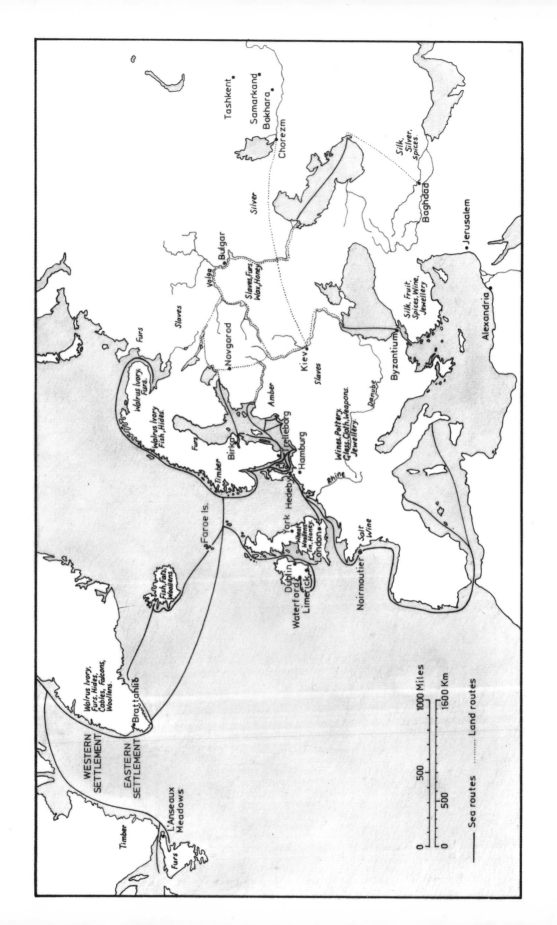

Tashkent

Samarkand

Bokhara

Chorezm

Silver

Silk, Silver, Spices

Baghdad

Jerusalem

Bulgar

Volga

Slaves

Slaves, Furs, Wax, Honey

Novgorod

Kiev

Slaves

Alexandria

Silk, Fruit, Spices, Wine, Jewellery

Byzantium

Furs

Walrus Ivory, Furs

Walrus Ivory, Fish, Hides

Amber

Furs

Birka

Grelleborg

Timber

Hamburg

Danube

Wines, Pottery, Glass, Cloth, Weapons, Jewellery

Faroe Is.

Rhine

York Hedeby

Wheat, Woollens, Tin, Honey

Dublin

London

Salt Wine

Waterford

Limerick

Noirmoutier

Fish, Fats, Woollens

WESTERN
SETTLEMENT

Walrus Ivory, Furs, Hides, Cables, Falcons, Woollens

EASTERN
SETTLEMENT

Brattahlið

Timber

L'Anseaux
Meadows

Furs

0   500   1000 Miles

0   500   1600 Km

————— Sea routes

·········· Land routes

Silver bracelets and neck rings from a Swedish hoard found at Asarve in the Baltic island of Gotland.

The pressure of land-shortage may well have been intensified by political pressure, for the ninth century saw a growth of royal power in Norway, culminating in the attempt by King Harald Fine-Hair to unify the whole country under one crown. But the early emigrants, one may assume, were younger sons frustrated by the law of primogeniture; brisk and vigorous men looking to make a livelihood elsewhere and not averse to the use of force if necessary, for piracy and cattle-raiding were endemic everywhere in those days.

In *The Age of the Vikings*, P. H. Sawyer sums up the Viking expansion as 'an extension of normal Dark Age activity, made possible and profitable by special circumstances'. The major factor in these 'special circumstances' was the technological revolution that produced the Viking sailing ship in the eighth century. And not just the warship. Just as significant in the story of Viking expansion was the merchant ship, the *knörr*, which followed in the wake of the first raiders and settlers. It was these deep-sea traders which pioneered the North Atlantic routes and consolidated the movement westwards.

The eastward movement by the Vikings was made by the Swedes. In the four centuries before the Viking Age began, Sweden had been growing rich on Baltic trade. Her wealth at this time has been amply

The trade routes of the Viking world

demonstrated by the magnificent grave-goods with which Swedish aristocrats were buried: Sweden had a Golden Age, in fact, before she had a Viking Age. Cities flourished, like Helgö on Lake Mälar, where archaeologists have found evidence of trade contacts with both Eastern and Western Europe, and perhaps even as far afield as India. With the onset of the Viking Age, the Swedes started to penetrate Russia in pursuit of the rich fur trade and the exotic markets of Persia and China. Swedish pioneers made their way across Russia by way of the major rivers and overland portages to the Caspian Sea and the Black Sea, founding trading centres as they went. By the ninth century, Swedes had reached Byzantium (Constantinople). Nearly 60,000 Arabic coins have now been unearthed in Scandinavia—striking evidence of the extent of the commerce that went on, and the amount of wealth that was flowing from the east into Scandinavia.

In Constantinople the Swedes joined the Varangian Guard, a kind of Byzantine Foreign Legion that attracted hundreds of Scandinavian mercenaries and soldiers of fortune. The Vikings called Russia *Garðaríki*—the kingdom of towns—or else *Svíþjóð hinn mikla* (Greater Sweden); and it is likely that the name Russia means 'the land of the Swedes', because contemporary Slav chronicles refer to the incomers who founded the great city states of Kiev and Novgorod as *Rus*, or *Rhos*, and these were in all probability Swedes. The Swedes never conquered Russia, and there is no archaeological evidence of dense Scandinavian settlements. They contented themselves with taking control of existing towns and creating new fortified trading centres along the river routes. They extorted tribute from neighbouring Slav tribes, and used it for trade, but they seem to have become assimilated and Slavicised quite quickly.

While the Swedes looked east, the Danes looked south-west along the northern coasts of Europe and towards England. They did not start off as would-be colonists, like the Norwegians, but as pirates attracted by the rich trade of Charlemagne's Frankish Empire. They often worked with official or unofficial royal backing, like the Elizabethan sea-dogs who battened on the bullion ships of the Spanish Main and became national heroes thereby. Later in the Viking Age, Danish designs on Europe, and especially England, became openly territorial: the flag followed the trade, just as trade had followed piracy.

In this book we are concerned mainly with the Norwegians and to a lesser extent with the Danes. Our canvas is the Viking expansion westwards, the great impetus that took the Norsemen to England,

Penannular bronze cloak pin from Gotland with gilt and silver decoration

Scotland, Ireland, the Faroes, Iceland, Greenland, and ultimately North America (*Vínland*). In the course of the journey we shall find a very different picture of the Vikings from the popular image of savage barbarians. Archaeology, and to a lesser extent the study of place-names and coins, has done much to correct this naïve conception. We know now that the Vikings brought to Europe a new vitality in a great variety of ways. They pioneered new trade routes across the known world, and extended the boundaries of that world by tireless exploration. They created new art-forms, new societies, new concepts of law and justice. They created a new nation, Iceland, that is still regarded as the oldest democracy in Europe.

In that new nation there arose one of the great literatures of medieval Europe: the literature of the sagas. From the twelfth and thirteenth centuries onwards, a great mass of narrative material was written down in prose form in Iceland. There were histories and homilies, translations of saints' lives and other works of ecclesiastical learning, treatises on geography and astronomy and exploration and grammar and poetry, folk-tales and science-fiction. Above all there were the so-called Family Sagas, stories about the great families who settled in Iceland and their descendants. And even though the official language of learning in those days was Latin, all this material was written in the vernacular, in Icelandic.

The Icelandic sagas and histories and other learned works are one of the major sources for our knowledge of the Viking Age. Originally they were thought of as literal historical truth throughout Scandinavia; then in the nineteenth century scepticism set in, and they were regarded as myths and fables. Today a more balanced view is possible. Like any other contemporary or near-contemporary documents they have to be interpreted with great care, for fact and fiction are sometimes difficult to distinguish. But without them, our archaeological picture of the Viking Age would be much the poorer.

In this book Icelandic names are given in the original, apart from dropping the nominatival ending (usually *-ur*) which is not a root part of the word itself. Icelandic uses accents not as stress marks but to affect the pronunciation of vowels, and it has three additional characters that will be unfamiliar to most people:

þ (Þ), a consonant called *thorn*, pronounced *th* as in *thing*.
ð (Ð), a consonant called *eth*, pronounced *th* as in *then*.
æ (Æ), a diphthong called *ash*, pronounced long *i* as in *life*.

The other major pronunciation changes are as follows:

á, pronounced *ow* as in *owl*.
é, pronounced *ye* as in *yet*.
í, pronounced *ee* as in *seen*.
ó, pronounced *oh* as in *Oh*.
ö, pronounced *eu* as in French *fleur*.
ú, pronounced *oo* as in *soon*.
ei, pronounced *ay* as in *tray*.
au, pronounced *œi* as in French *œil*.

There are various other differences of pronunciation, particularly for double consonants, but with these basic vowel sounds one can get a reasonable impression of the names of the people who made possible the last stages of the Viking expansion westwards.

1

The Vikings in England

Just off the coast of Northumberland, in the north-east of England, lies a small tidal island called the Holy Island of Lindisfarne, linked to the mainland by a three-mile causeway across the sand-flats. Today it contains little but a village, the remains of a small sixteenth-century castle, and the ruins of a twelfth-century Benedictine priory.

When the ruined priory was being restored about fifty years ago, a curious fragment of carved stone was found in it, evidently dating from the end of the eighth century. On one side are various Christian symbols—the Cross, the sun and the moon, God's hands, and worshippers at prayer. On the other side a line of Viking warriors advances in single file, brandishing swords and battle-axes, wearing heavy jerkins and tight-fitting trousers. This stone, now in the museum on Lindisfarne, is a witness to the earliest recorded Viking onslaught on England—a sudden raid on the Holy Island of Lindisfarne on June 8, 793 AD. It was the prelude to 250 years of Scandinavian invasion of England.

Lindisfarne had been a peaceful sanctuary of Christian culture since the middle of the seventh century, when a company of Celtic missionaries from the Scottish island of Iona founded a monastery there. One of its most celebrated bishops was St Cuthbert, to whom the church was dedicated. It was here that the magnificent illuminated book known as the Lindisfarne Gospels, now in the British Museum, was produced by Bishop Eadfrith around the year 700.

The raid on Lindisfarne by prowling Norwegians in 793 shook the Christian world. It was vividly described in the *Anglo-Saxon Chronicle*, a compilation of annals first produced in Wessex at the end of the ninth century under King Alfred the Great. Thus, the

entry for 793 was not recorded until a full century after the event:

'793. In this year terrible portents appeared over Northumbria and sorely affrighted the inhabitants; these were exceptional flashes of lightning, and fiery dragons were seen flying in the air. A great famine followed soon upon these signs, and a little after that in the same year on the ides of June the harrying of the heathen miserably destroyed God's church on Lindisfarne by rapine and slaughter.'

Christian writers were quick to interpret the Viking assault as a punishment for sins. The Northumbrian scholar-priest Alcuin, who was at that time living in France as an adviser to the Emperor Charlemagne, sent letters to Northumbria expressing his horror at this act of divine retribution that had come almost literally as a bolt from the blue:

'Lo, it is some 350 years that we and our forefathers have inhabited this most lovely land, and never before has such a terror appeared in Britain as we have now suffered from a pagan race, nor was it thought possible that such an inroad from the sea could be made. Behold the church of St Cuthbert spattered with the blood of the priests of God, despoiled of all its ornaments; a place more venerable than all in Britain is given as a prey to pagan peoples.'

Almost right away, the Vikings had been cast in the role of anti-Christ. By the twelfth century the chronicler Simeon of Durham was using even more lurid language to describe this raid:

'In the same year [793] the pagans from the northern regions came with a fleet of ships to Britain like stinging hornets and spreading on all sides like fearful wolves, robbed, tore and slaughtered not only beasts of burden, sheep and oxen, but even priests and deacons, and companies of monks and nuns. And they came to the Church of Lindisfarne, laid everything waste with grievous plundering, trampled the holy places with polluted steps, dug up the altars and seized all the treasures of the holy church. They killed some of the brothers, took some away with them in fetters, many they drove out, naked and loaded with insults, some they drowned in the sea.'

The accounts have clearly become exaggerated by ecclesiastical outrage and pious shock, for enough monks survived to keep the monastery going and to carve the stone commemorating the attack. It was not until 875, almost a century later, that they finally abandoned the island, fearing renewed assaults from the Danish army that was by that time overrunning East Anglia, Mercia, and Northumbria. And not all the ornaments could have been despoiled, as Alcuin and Simeon of Durham had claimed, for when the monks eventually left they took with them the precious Lindisfarne Gospels, and the coffin of St Cuthbert (now in Durham Cathedral) crammed with as many church treasures as they could carry.

When the Church was not directly involved, the accounts of the early clashes are much more restrained. About the same time as the attack on Lindisfarne, or even a year or two earlier, there was a quayside brawl at Portland on the Dorset coast during which the sheriff of Dorset and his retinue were killed. In the *Anglo-Saxon Chronicle* entry for 789, which covered the events of the reign of King Brihtic of Wessex (786–802), this scuffle gets only a brief and unimpassioned notice:

'789. . . . A small fleet of Danes, numbering three fast ships, came unexpectedly to the coast, and this was their first coming. Hearing of this the king's official, then staying at the town called Dorchester, leapt on his horse and with a few men made haste to the port, thinking they were merchants rather than enemies, and commanding them imperiously he ordered them to be sent to the royal villa, but he and his companions were straightway killed by them. The name of the official was Beaduheard.' (*Æthelweard version*)

Here there is none of the hysterical alarm that greeted the news of Lindisfarne. Indeed, it suggests that there had already been contacts

Viking warriors
on board ship.
From carvings on
the Gotland
picture-stones

The British Isles in
the Viking Age

of a peaceful commercial kind between Scandinavia and England
before the Viking Age. Other versions of the *Anglo-Saxon Chronicle*
describe the strangers at Portland as coming from the south-west of
Norway. The initial raids, in fact, seem to have been made exclusively
by Norwegians.

The first attacks were sporadic and seem to have been less effective
than the chroniclers would suggest. They can be seen as preliminary
forays to find the weakest and most profitable points in the coastal
defences, and these happened to be the rich and isolated island
monasteries. Already, Norwegian settlers had started moving into
the Northern Isles and the Hebrides in Scotland (see Chapter 2),
and the early raids seem to have been offshoots of this migration.

Thus, in 794, the year after the Lindisfarne raid, Vikings attacked and plundered another monastery in Northumbria, perhaps Jarrow, where the Venerable Bede had written his celebrated *Ecclesiastical History* earlier in the eighth century; but this time one of their leaders was killed and some of their ships were wrecked in a storm with heavy loss of life. The following year, in 795, St Columba's monastery on Iona, the mother church of Celtic monasticism in Scotland, was looted, and again in 802 and 806; and also in 795 came the first recorded raid on Ireland, with an attack on the island of Reachrainn, somewhere off the east coast. By 799 the first raiders were reported on various islands off the Aquitaine coast of France.

In this last decade of the eighth century the Viking raids in the west had thus begun in earnest. Throughout the ninth century they were to affect the whole seaboard of Western Europe, and Viking expeditions would work their way around Spain and through the Straits of Gibraltar into the Mediterranean. But for the time being, England was able to draw breath again; for after the initial forays against Northumbria, there are no records of further attacks until 835—and this time the Vikings came mainly from Denmark, and came in strength.

Throughout the years of the Frankish Empire under Charlemagne (771–814), the Danes had been hungrily eyeing the wealth behind its defended borders. Denmark was a much more organised kingdom in the military sense than Norway at this time, and when the Frankish Empire started breaking up under Charlemagne's son, Louis the Pious, the Danes struck.

The first major onslaught on Frisia (modern Holland) was launched in 834, when a Danish expedition attacked the prosperous trading centre of Dorestad (Duurstede), south-east of Utrecht. It lay on a branch of the Rhine, and was the largest market town in northern Europe. It was heavily fortified but it failed to withstand the assault, and for a generation thereafter it was systematically plundered, year after year.

The attack on Dorestad opened the floodgates. In the following year, 835, the first Danish marauders attacked England, when 'the heathen devastated Sheppey', a small island in the Thames. From this time onwards, Viking expeditions by both Danes and Norwegians on both sides of the English Channel went hand in hand.

In that same year, 835, the island of Noirmoutier, a monastic site and trading centre for salt and wine at the mouth of the Loire, was attacked. A few years later, in 842, came a memorable raid on the

Viking warriors on board ship. From carvings on the Gotland picture-stones

town of Nantes, farther up the Loire, which was thoroughly documented by contemporary French chroniclers. It seems that Viking bands were now being used as mercenaries in the internal politics of France, where Count Lambert had rebelled against Charlemagne's grandson, Charles the Bald. Guided by French pilots in the pay of Count Lambert, a large Norwegian fleet slipped up the Loire and fell upon Nantes on June 24, when the town was crowded with celebrants for the Feast of St John the Baptist. A terrible massacre ensued. Count Lambert won Nantes, while the Vikings withdrew to the island of Noirmoutier to settle for the winter 'as if they meant to stay for ever'. And thus began a new pattern for the raids: they were no longer simply a matter of seasonal employment for mettlesome young men with time on their hands in the slack of the agricultural year. Raiding had become a way of life.

In England the new pattern began in 850, when for the first time Danish Vikings wintered on the island of Thanet, in the Thames, and again in 855 on the island of Sheppey. No traces of the fortifications they must have put up have been identified so far, but the use of winter bases in England became more and more common.

On the continent suddenly, it seemed, there were Vikings everywhere. Ermentarius of Noirmoutier described the chaos with fulsome eloquence in the 860s:

'The number of ships increases, the endless flood of Vikings never ceases to grow bigger. Everywhere Christ's people are the victims of massacre, burning and plunder. The Vikings overrun all that lies before them, and none can withstand them. They seize Bordeaux, Périgueux, Limôges, Angoulême, Toulouse; Angers, Tours, and Orléans are made deserts. Ships past counting voyage up the Seine, and throughout the entire region evil grows strong.'

Up the Seine in 845 had come a Danish Viking called Ragnar, under royal orders from the King of Denmark to capture Paris. This Ragnar has come to be associated with one of the most celebrated Vikings of popular legend—Ragnar Hairy-Breeks (*loðbrók*). Ragnar Hairy-Breeks belongs more to the world of fable than to history. He was the hero of a legendary saga which was immensely popular throughout Scandinavia, according to which he was put to death in a snake-pit in York by King Ella of Northumbria with a smile and a heroic lay on his lips. Whether he ever existed at all is a matter of some doubt, but his hold on the popular imagination is indestructible.

Whatever the truth about this picturesquely-named character,

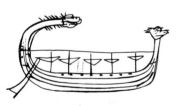

Viking ship carved on a rune stick. Bergen, thirteenth century

history records that the mission up the Seine in 845 was successful. Ragnar duly ransacked Paris, whereupon the Emperor Charles the Bald paid him 7,000 pounds of silver to go away in peace.

This was the first recorded instance of a policy that was to become commonplace in later English history—the payment of Danegeld (Danes' Pay) to buy off the raiders. It was a tactic of dubious value, for though it might buy a temporary respite it could also become a tempting source of easy revenue for freelance raiders. In 865 a Danish force arrived in Thanet and made an agreement with the men of Kent to go away—no doubt after payment of Danegeld.

But the year 865 also saw a more serious development, with the arrival in England of what the *Anglo-Saxon Chronicle* calls the Great Heathen Horde. In his book *The Age of the Vikings*, P. H. Sawyer has suggested that the *Chronicle* invariably exaggerated the size of the marauding Viking bands, perhaps in order to enhance the achievements of the English defenders; this Great Heathen Horde probably numbered no more than five hundred or at most a thousand men. Three brothers are named as leaders—Ivar the Boneless, Ubbi, and Halfdan, the sons of the Ragnar who had captured Paris. According to legend, of course, they were the sons of none other than Ragnar Hairy-Breeks, who with his dying breath in the snake-pit at York was alleged to have said, 'The piglets would be grunting if they knew the plight of the boar.' The piglets had now arrived, intent on vengeance.

The Great Horde marched north, where Northumbria was in the throes of civil war—it was not only the Vikings who were responsible for the turbulence of the age—and in 867 they captured York. Legend alone records the exultant and savage vengeance inflicted on King Ella—Ragnar's sons are said to have carved the blood-eagle on his back. This cruel ritual, which seems to have been rare in practice, involved cutting the victim's ribs from his spine, pulling out his lungs, and spreading them on his back like wings as a sacrifice to the god Óðin. The barbarity of rituals of this kind, like the misconception that the Vikings drank toasts from the skulls of their enemies, did much to popularise the Vikings amongst the thrill-seeking Romantic revivalists of the nineteenth century.

For ten years the Great Horde ranged through Northumbria, East Anglia and Wessex until the army began to split up and colonise the conquered kingdoms. In 875 Halfdan divided out the lands of the Northumbrians among his warriors and they began to farm them, while he himself set off for further military adventures in Ireland, where he died two years later. He left the Great Horde depleted, and an area approximating to Yorkshire firmly settled by Vikings-turned-farmers—the first part of England to be actively colonised. Two years later the Danes partitioned and settled Mercia, and soon afterwards did the same in East Anglia. In this way the major part of the Great Horde took root in England.

The remainder, under a new leader, Guthrum, found it hard to make further headway. By now King Alfred was on the throne of Wessex, the only king in English history to be graced with the title of 'the Great'. His reign started inauspiciously, for after some early set-backs he was forced to take refuge in the marshes of Athelney, a fugitive king without an army. It was here that a peevish housewife was said to have scolded him for failing to prevent her cakes from burning when he was left to look after them—a charming story that symbolises both his preoccupation with the destiny of England and the low ebb of his own fortunes. In the event, Alfred managed to build up his military strength sufficiently to drive the Danes out of Wessex and recapture London from them. The climax of his patient campaigning came in 886 when he concluded a treaty with Guthrum, in which the partition of England was formally recognised. It was the first official definition of the southern limits of the Danish-controlled regions to the north of a line stretching roughly from the Thames to Liverpool, that came to be known as the Danelaw. The treaty gave the Scandinavians the right to settle in the north of England, and in the areas of the Five Boroughs—Nottingham, Lincoln, Stamford, Derby and Leicester.

For the next fifty years the Danelaw was a significant and separate political entity encompassing half of England. With their accumulated treasure from years of campaigning, the Scandinavian settlers, both Danes and Norwegians, gave the whole area a welcome economic stimulus. Apart from some sculptured stones, little archaeological evidence from this period has been unearthed as yet; but the newcomers brought with them a distinctive Scandinavian flavour which had a lasting effect on English society.

The *Anglo-Saxon Chronicle* entry for 878 suggests that when the Danes invaded the land of the West Saxons in that year, they 'drove a great part of the people over the sea and conquered most of the others' before King Alfred rallied his forces and pushed them into East Anglia. Many of the native estate-owners must have been dispossessed, certainly, but there is nothing to suggest that the Anglo-Saxons were exterminated or enslaved or driven away in any great numbers. The two peoples were soon living together in amity.

Penny minted by Alfred the Great in London.

Indeed, the Danes quickly made themselves popular with at least one section of the native population: a contemporary writer, John of Wallingford, complained that the Danes were always combing their hair and changing their underwear, and took baths regularly on Saturdays, which gave them an unfair advantage over their Anglo-Saxon rivals with the local maidens.

The incomers seem to have adopted the Anglo-Saxon open-field system of agriculture, while further north the Norwegian settlers took to rearing sheep in the uplands, as they had done at home. They were not content simply to take over existing farms; with the extra capital at their disposal, they moved vigorously into land that had not been previously exploited for farming. The peasant small-holders of the Danelaw, each with their 25 acres and a couple of cows, were the backbone of the community; indeed the Danelaw society has been described as a peasant aristocracy.

The Danelaw was divided into administrative districts called *wapentakes*. This word refers to the 'weapon-taking' or 'weapon-brandishing' by which decisions were confirmed at the local assemblies, or *Things* as they were called, and later it came to mean the district from which members of a Thing were drawn. These local Things were an established feature in their homeland, and were attended by all freeholding farmers under a presiding Lawman.

The Danes also brought their own legal codes and institutions. It was they, for instance, who introduced the word law into the English language. In the Danelaw, the compensation to be paid for killing a man (*wergild*) depended on the status of the victim, whereas in Anglo-Saxon England it depended on the status of the victim's master—an important distinction involving differing concepts of freedom and equality. It was the Danes, too, who created in their local courts at the Things the forerunner of the English jury system and the principle of majority jury verdicts: twelve freeholders were sworn not to accuse an innocent man nor to shield a guilty one.

The great number of Scandinavian place-names in the Danelaw reveals how deeply the incomers took root. Today there are at least seven hundred places in England which include the element -*by*, which was Scandinavian for village or farm, and which still survives in modern English in the word by-law, meaning a town or village local regulation or law.

The English language as a whole was much affected, because the basis of modern English is the East Midland dialect where Danes and Anglo-Saxons intermingled most closely. Old Norse and Old

Axonometric reconstruction of wattle-and-post houses at Hedeby

English were closely related languages, but not so alike that the settlers and the natives could understand one another readily. A kind of pidgin English developed, into which the Scandinavians introduced a host of new words, and affected the syntax, the pronunciation, and even the grammar of English itself.

The incomers took over the major Anglo-Saxon towns and villages as a dominant minority, and created many new secondary settlements of their own. They had been used to urban life as well as agriculture in their homeland, and it is possible that the original army veterans who were given land in the Danelaw were later reinforced by new immigrants, particularly merchants. Towns and trading centres had been growing rapidly in Denmark throughout the ninth century. The largest of these, Hedeby, at the neck of the Jutland peninsula south of Slesvig where it joins Germany, was built just after 800. Strategically placed on the shore of Haddeby Noor, a lake at the head of the River Schlei, it soon became an important commercial staging-post on the trade route from Frisia to the towns of the Baltic.

Hedeby was fortified on the landward side by a huge semicircular earthen rampart, thirty feet high in places. This great earthwork survived the eventual destruction of the town by King Harald Hard-Ruler (*harðráði*) of Norway in the 1050s, and attracted the attention of the earliest Scandinavian antiquarians in the sixteenth century. The Viking town itself, which covered some sixty acres, has been systematically excavated by the German archaeologists Herbert Jankuhn and Kurt Schietzel, and now provides a clear and detailed picture of what urban life in Viking times was like.

It was a rather untidily laid out town, with two main roads running through it at right angles. For the rest, shops, barns, stables, storage sheds and houses stood side by side without much attempt at organisation, although the merchants' houses were enclosed by palisades of plaited hurdles. The whole town revolved around commerce. There was a ship-repairing yard down by the shore. One area of wooden houses seems to have been a craftsmen's quarter, in which pottery-making, iron-smelting, weaving, bronze-casting and glass-making were carried on. But these local products were of secondary importance to the immense luxury trade that passed through Hedeby to avoid the perilous, pirate-haunted sea journey round Jutland. From the Baltic, valuable furs and slaves flowed west, from Europe came textiles and wines and jewellery and fine pottery and glassware.

Compared with the older, more sophisticated cities of continental Europe, life in Hedeby must have been rather rough and ready, like some permanent frontier town. In 950 a Spanish Moor called Al-Tartushi returned to his native Cordoba after a stay in Hedeby and left a distinctly unflattering account of the conditions:

> 'They hold festivals where they assemble to honour their god and to eat and drink. Whoever sacrifices an animal sets up a pole in front of his door and hangs the slaughtered animal on it . . . The town is poorly off for goods and wealth, the people live mostly on fish, of which there is plenty, and if anyone has a child there it is thrown into the sea to save the expense of bringing it up. Women there have the right to declare themselves divorced whenever they please. . . . Never did I hear more hideous singing than that of the people of Slesvig; it is like a growl in the throat, like the barking of dogs, only much more beastly.'

Despite the patronising comments of the fastidious Arab, Hedeby had its own mint. A silver coin found at the important Swedish trading town of Birka was probably struck in Hedeby early in the ninth century. Soon the Scandinavians, who had no international coinage of their own, were minting coins of English type and weight within the Danelaw. It is a clear indication of the way in which the Danelaw settled down into a semi-urbanised Viking community.

Christianity was accepted by the incomers in their own easy-going fashion. Very few pagan Viking graves have been found from this period; the largest Viking cemetery found so far is at Ingleby in Derbyshire, comprising sixty relatively small grave-mounds covering cremation-burials which in some cases had been quite richly furnished. It was not a Christian custom to bury the dead with their personal belongings. Guthrum himself had accepted baptism in the course of his negotiations with King Alfred, but this was no doubt for reasons of political expediency rather than piety. Far from being

A carved stone cross from Middleton in Yorkshire. *Left* the Viking is laid with his weapons beside him; *right* the ornamentation on the back echoes the Jellinge style.

anti-Christian, the Vikings were quite prepared to accept Christ into their own loose pantheon of gods.

One of the stone crosses from Middleton, in Yorkshire, carved in the last quarter of the ninth century, demonstrates this comfortable adaptability. The stone cross itself is a Christian symbol, but the carving represents a typically pagan burial, with a helmeted Viking warrior laid to rest with his weapons beside him—a spear at his right hand, his shield, sword and axe at his left, and his *sax*, or long knife, across his body.

The reverse side of the cross is an early example of the impact of the vigorous art-forms the Vikings introduced wherever they went. The native sculptor has tried, not too successfully, to graft onto his own work elements of the so-called Jellinge style, which developed in Scandinavia in the middle of the ninth century. It is characterised by ribbon-like animals entwined in interlace, and takes its name from the finds at the royal cemetery at Jelling, in Jutland—particularly the magnificently carved Jelling Stone which was set up around 980 by King Harald Gormsson of Denmark (Harald Blue-Tooth) in memory of his parents.

The establishment of the Danelaw in 886 did not bring automatic peace to England. A new Viking threat appeared in 892 when a large army came by sea from Boulogne whence it had been driven by famine on the continent. After wandering rather fruitlessly through the western parts of England it, too, settled down. The *Anglo-Saxon Chronicle* records:

> '896. And afterwards in the summer of this year the Danish army divided, one part going into East Anglia and one into Northumbria, and those that were without money [property?] got themselves ships and went south across the sea to the Seine . . .
>
> 'By the grace of God, the army had not on the whole afflicted the English people very greatly, but they were much more seriously afflicted by the mortality of cattle and men, and most of all in that many of the king's best thanes who were in the land died in these three years.'

This sober note is a reminder that the destructiveness commonly attributed to the Vikings by annalists and churchmen was much exaggerated. The Vikings were more interested in treasure and provisions, or in extorting tribute or protection money instead, than in destruction for its own sake. The damage they caused was incidental to the robbery, and was no worse than the normal acts of piracy and assault which were common practice at the time.

The Danes in the Danelaw did not turn all their swords into ploughshares at once. There are many reports of raids in the south and west by bands from within the Danelaw, both by land and sea, and King Alfred was at times hard pressed to contain them. He built a navy to defend the south coast, and a line of fortified boroughs along the boundaries of the Danelaw. Gradually these strongholds became bases for counter-attacks, and the process of recovering the occupied areas began under Alfred's son, Edward the Elder (died 924). Year by year, fortified boroughs were established deeper and

deeper into Danish-held territory. By the year 918 the whole of the Danelaw south of the Humber had been brought back under English rule.

Now the only independent Viking enclave left in Scandinavian hands was the kingdom of York. The North had always been a Norwegian as opposed to a Danish domain, and it remained a very different kind of settlement from those south of the Humber: more violent, less stable, rather like the difference, in fact, between Norway and Denmark, both in landscape and way of life. The mountainous and rugged countryside of the north of England was not unlike that of Norway, where huge physical barriers made any kind of real political unity difficult to maintain and the royal writ all but impossible to enforce. Norway bred a more independent, self-reliant race of Vikings who brooked no overlords.

Although York nominally submitted to King Edward the Elder in 920, it continued to be a cockpit of Norse ambitions for many years. Edward's successor, Æthelstan, one of the greatest warrior-kings of Anglo-Saxon England, kept up the pressure on the Scandinavians, and in 937 he confronted and defeated a powerful Norse-Celtic confederacy at the Battle of Brunanburh, somewhere in Northumbria. The site of the battle has never been positively identified, but it was remembered as one of the fiercest encounters ever to take place on English soil. Æthelstan and his brother Edmund, leading the armies of Wessex and Mercia, faced an alliance of Vikings from Ireland under King Olaf Guthfrithsson, of Scots under King Constantine, and Welshmen from Strathclyde in Scotland under Eugenius; by nightfall the Vikings and their allies had been routed after a day of terrible slaughter.

There is a wonderfully vivid description of the battle and its aftermath in one of the greatest of the Icelandic sagas, *Egil's Saga*, which was written early in the thirteenth century, nearly three hundred years after the event. The hero of the saga is the great Icelandic warrior-poet Egil Skallagrímsson, and he and his brother took part in the battle as freelance Vikings—on the winning English side. In the saga the site of the battle is called *Vínheiði*, and the date 937 is difficult to reconcile with the saga chronology, but there can be no doubt that they were one and the same action. Egil's brother was killed in the battle, which left Egil in no mood for the victory celebration held by King Æthelstan. Egil buried his brother in the pagan fashion, heaping his body with treasures, and then came stalking into the hall, beetle-browed, menacing, savage in his grief:

Crucifixion scene on the massive Jelling Stone in Denmark, which gave its name to the Jellinge style.

31

'Egil sat down on the high-seat on the lower dais, opposite the king, and thrust his shield in front of his legs. He was wearing a helmet, and he laid his sword across his knees, and every now and again he drew it halfway out and slammed it back into the scabbard. He sat bolt upright, but his head was bent low . . . And as he sat there, he twitched one eyebrow down onto his cheek and the other up into the roots of his wolf-grey hair. He refused to drink anything he was offered, and just twitched his eyebrows, now up, now down.

'King Æthelstan was sitting in his high-seat. He too had laid his sword across his knees. And when they had been sitting facing each other like this for a time, the king drew his sword from his scabbard. Then he took a big, handsome gold ring from his arm and hung it on the point of his sword. He stood up and walked out onto the floor, and reached across the fire with it towards Egil. Egil stood up and pulled out his sword and walked out onto the floor. He placed the point of his sword through the ring and drew it towards himself, and then went back to his place. The king returned to his high-seat. When Egil sat down he clasped the ring round his own arm, and with that his eyebrows fell into line . . .'

This coin minted at York by King Sigtrygg One-Eye (921–6) has a cross on one side and a sword on the other.

However garbled the details of the preceding battle may have become, few saga incidents can equal the power of that scene.

King Æthelstan died two years later; and despite the crushing victory he had won at Brunanburh, Norse kings ruled in York again, one after the other, precariously and chaotically, for nearly twenty years. The last in the line was the notorious Eirik Blood-Axe (*blóðöxi*), who had been forced from the throne of Norway for excessive cruelty.

The great number and variety of coins struck at York by these Norse kings in the first half of the tenth century bear witness to the confusion of the times. One silver coin minted in 915 bears what seems to be the emblem of Thór's Hammer, a pagan amulet, whereas the coinage of Sigtrygg One-Eye (921–6) has a Christian cross. His son Olaf Kvaran, who divided his time between Dublin and York with changing fortunes, favoured a neat Christian symbol during his third reign in York (942–52), whereas Eirik Blood-Axe, not surprisingly perhaps, featured a sword on his coinage during his last years at York (952–4).

These last two years were enlivened by the reappearance of the redoubtable Egil Skallagrímsson from Iceland. Egil was the prototype Viking of his age: warrior and poet, brave and greedy, a commoner impatient of royal authority. He had defied King Eirik Blood-Axe in Norway, and now he fell into the king's clutches by accident in York. But Egil escaped with his life, by composing an apparently impromptu eulogy in Eirik's honour, a poem known as the Head-Ransom (*Höfuðlausn*):

> 'Sword-metal pealed
> On rim of shield;
> Strife round him reeled
> Who ranged that field.
> Heard was the yell
> Of blade-fury fell,
> Iron-storm's knell
> Past far sea's swell . . .'

A sword is featured again on the coinage minted at York by Eirik Blood-Axe in his last years there.

As stanza followed clashing stanza, it became clear that Egil had introduced a revolutionary new element into the highly stylised alliterative court poetry of the North—the element of end-rhyme, which he must have heard in the Latin church litanies of his Christian hosts. It was striking evidence of the way in which Anglo-Saxon and Scandinavian cultures fertilised one another; and so electrifying was the effect in that hall in York that Eirik Blood-Axe spared his enemy, knowing that his own immortality was assured in that one poem.

Eirik Blood-Axe was finally expelled from York in 954. He was betrayed, it seems, at Stainmore, and killed after a valiant defence. England was a single united kingdom at last. The end of the Norwegian kingdom of York was to prove the end of one Viking era—but not the last.

After Eirik's expulsion and death England enjoyed twenty-five years of respite from Viking attacks under strong kings like Edgar (959–75). But in 978 a twelve-year-old boy came to the throne; his name was Æthelred, and during his feeble-handed reign (978–1013) he was to earn the eloquent title of 'Unready' (*Unræd*, meaning 'lacking in counsel'). Across the North Sea the Vikings scented weakness and easy profit, and turned their prows towards England again.

The first Viking leader to make his mark was Olaf Tryggvason, who had been reared on piracy in the Baltic and who aspired to the throne of Norway itself. According to one version of the *Anglo-Saxon Chronicle*, it was Olaf Tryggvason who commanded the Norse army at the Battle of Maldon on August 10, 991. It took place on the island of Northey in the estuary of the River Blackwater, and although it was a relatively insignificant encounter between the Vikings and the East Saxons, it was immortalised in an almost contemporary Anglo-Saxon poem, *The Battle of Maldon*—the last and perhaps the finest literary flowering of the heroic spirit of the age. It tells of the defeat and death of the brave Ealdorman of Essex, Byrhtnoth, and how his men vowed to avenge their leader or seek their own death in battle:

> 'Zeal shall be the fiercer, heart the keener,
> Courage the greater, as our strength lessens.'

Ealdorman Byrhtnoth was the last true Anglo-Saxon hero, but his stand was unavailing. Olaf Tryggvason concluded a treaty with Æthelred the Unready: in return for a Danegeld payment of £10,000 the Vikings were to depart in peace and to respect all English ships abroad, while foreign merchant ships in English waters were to be guaranteed immunity from attack.

Olaf left England, but part of his band remained to continue the looting; and in 994 Olaf Tryggvason returned. This time he had ninety-four ships behind him, it was claimed, and at his side the King of Denmark, the shrewd and patient strategist who was to become the first Danish king to conquer all England—Svein Fork-Beard (983–1014), son of King Harald Gormsson of Jelling fame. Together Olaf and Svein Fork-Beard launched a determined attack on London, but London held out, and instead the Vikings plundered the south-east regions and accepted from Æthelred the Unready a bribe of £16,000 to go away. Svein Fork-Beard returned

A manuscript illumination in the Icelandic *Flateyjarbók* depicts Olaf Tryggvason, victor at the Battle of Maldon and later King of Norway.

to Denmark to mature his plans for the eventual conquest of England, while Olaf Tryggvason, that fierce and ruthless Viking, was baptised in the Scilly Isles and went back to seize the throne of Norway in 995. He was to reign for only five energetic years, and earn himself an unlikely reputation as the blood-and-iron warrior king for Christ.

Prompted by the scheming brain of Svein Fork-Beard in Denmark, the invasions continued unabated. The price of peace escalated as the amounts of Danegeld paid by King Æthelred rose. Svein Fork-Beard returned in person in 1003, allegedly to avenge the death of a sister slaughtered in an attempted massacre by King Æthelred of all the Danes in the Danelaw in 1002. England sagged and cracked under the annual onslaughts, demoralisation and disorganisation were everywhere, and in 1007 Æthelred paid out £36,000 for peace.

The invasions were now different from those of the previous century. They were no longer conducted by freebooting adventurers intent only on plunder, to be followed up by more or less peaceful settlement. They were now well-planned expeditions led by kings and princes for political and financial gain. In 1009, for instance, it was another would-be king of Norway, Olaf Haraldsson (St Olaf, who reigned from 1014–30), who tore down London Bridge with his grappling irons and thus gave birth to the nursery rhyme 'London Bridge is falling down'.

The men who took part in these massive expeditions were now professional soldiers and mercenaries. At the end of the tenth century there was a number of fortified strongholds in Denmark which could serve as forts of refuge, but may also have been used as barracks for King Svein Fork-Beard's armies of invasion.

Four of these military bases have been excavated by archaeologists: at Trelleborg on the west coast of Zealand, Nonnebakken under the city of Odense on the island of Fyn, Fyrkat in East Jutland, and Aggersborg in North Jutland. All of them were built and occupied between 970 and 1020. Much the largest of them was Aggersborg, which could accommodate some 3,000 troops; but the one that has been most fully published is Trelleborg.

Trelleborg stands in a good defensive position, surrounded by towering earthen ramparts fifty-nine feet thick and twenty-three feet high, reinforced in places by a deep ditch. It was laid out with great military precision, unlike the town of Hedeby. From the four gateways at the four points of the compass, two arrow-straight streets paved with timber intersected at right angles to divide the internal area of the camp into four equal quadrants. Each quadrant con-

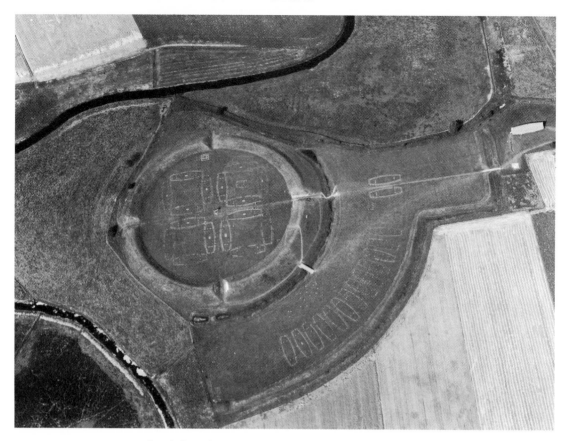

Aerial view of Trelleborg, one of the great Viking fortresses in Denmark.

tained four barrack-houses nearly a hundred feet long, arranged in a hollow square (the post-holes are visible to this day), making sixteen in all.

Each barrack-house had curved sides and a hipped roof, with walls of vertical wooden planks, divided into three rooms. The central room had a fire down the middle of the floor, and a dais along each longitudinal wall on which the soldiery sprawled at their ease and made up their beds at night. On the archaeological evidence they were kept scrupulously tidy; no discarded weapons were found. These could have been the winter quarters for 1200 men of Svein Fork-Beard's army of conquest, and served also to house the garrisons guarding Denmark when he was away on imperial business.

Ironically enough it was the English themselves who paid for their own conquest. The huge sums of Danegeld levied from the tax-payers ended up by financing the Viking invasions, for they were used by their leaders to pay their men, and vast quantities of Anglo-Saxon silver coins have been found in hoards abroad, particularly in Sweden.

Swedish mercenaries, in fact, seemed to have played a large part in these invasions, and one memorial rune-stone at Orkestad in Uppland tells the whole story in one terse epitaph:

'Karsi and Gerbjörn had this stone raised in memory of Úlf their father. God and God's Mother help his soul. And Úlf received Danegeld three times in England. The first was that which Tosti paid. Then Thorkel paid. Then Knút paid.'

The names of the paymasters on the rune-stone summarise the years of the Danish conquest. 'Tosti' is not now readily identifiable.

A memorial rune-stone at Orkestad in Sweden tells of three expeditions against England, and the men who led them.

An eleventh-century carved stone found in the churchyard of St Paul's Cathedral, London, shows the influence of the Ringerike style from Scandinavia.

But 'Thorkel' was Thorkel the Tall (*hávi*), Svein Fork-Beard's lieutenant, one of the leaders of a great invasion fleet in 1009 which was bought off after three years of plundering for the staggering sum of £48,000. And 'Knút' was the great Knút himself (Canute), first and only king of a North Sea empire that embraced both Scandinavia and England.

It was Svein Fork-Beard who made it possible. After his long years of watchful planning, he had arrived in England in July, 1013, to deal the coup-de-grâce to Æthelred's tottering throne. By Christmas, Æthelred had fled to kinsmen in Normandy and King Svein was master of all England. He lived only five more weeks to enjoy his new realm. But when he died on February 3, 1014 he had by his side his younger son Knút, then aged about eighteen; and it took this young man only two years to deal with Æthelred's successor, the short-lived Edmund Ironside, and have himself declared King of England. Within another ten years, by diligent attention to Scandinavian affairs, he had inherited the crown of Denmark from his brother and made himself king of Norway and part of Sweden. Under Knút, the high point of Viking imperialism in the west was reached.

He brought to England twenty years of sorely-needed peace and a careful code of law that emphasised justice and the proper rights of individuals. From Scandinavia flowed a last flourishing of Viking art to reinvigorate the native styles—the so-called Ringerike style that emerged at the end of the tenth century, characterised by a lion-type animal and snake with flowing tendrils. It is seen on the finely-carved stone slab from the churchyard of St Paul's Cathedral in London and now in the Guildhall Museum; it depicts a backward-looking animal elaborately entwined by a snake. A decorated bone pin found in the Thames and now in the British Museum shows complete mastery by an Anglo-Saxon craftsman of this new Viking style, as does a fragment of a tombstone from Otley in Yorkshire.

Today Knút, or Canute, is perhaps best known to popular folklore as the king who tried to command the tide not to come in. In the Icelandic *Knýtlinga Saga* (Saga of the Knút Dynasty) he is described as having been tall and strong and fair-haired, with handsome features only marred by a long and slightly bent nose: 'He was a man of great good luck in everything to do with power.'

The luck did not run in his family. When he died in 1035 his North Sea empire was divided among his sons, who quickly proved themselves incompetent to manage their patrimony. Within a few years England had slipped from the Scandinavian crown when the English elected Æthelred's son, Edward the Confessor, to the throne in 1042, and the rest of the empire quickly disintegrated. The tide of Viking power had finally turned.

Only one last throw remained. In January 1066, Edward the Confessor died and the English promptly acclaimed their military leader, Harold Godwinsson, as king. But two foreign rulers of Viking blood had their own eyes on the throne.

In Normandy, Duke William the Bastard was the descendant of the Viking adventurers who had so sorely afflicted the continent in the first century of the Viking raids. A Norwegian freebooter with the picturesque name of Göngu-Hrólf (Ganger-Rolf, or Rolf the Walker, so called because he was so big that no horse could carry him) had unsuccessfully besieged Chartres in 911, but then acquired by the treaty of St Clair-sur-Epte from King Charles the Simple of France the rolling agricultural lands of Normandy. His name has come down to history as Rollo, the first and only Viking leader to establish a permanent Norse presence on the continent. His Norman descendants were still the Northmen, or *Normenn*, of former times, their adventurous energy now blended with the traditional adminis-

An English manuscript
drawing of King
Knút and his consort
shows them placing a
gold cross on the altar
of Winchester
Cathedral.

trative skills of France to form the most powerful feudal principality on the continent. Duke William was the outstanding example of this genetic mixture, a hundred and fifty years later; and although his rights were tenuous, he now asserted a claim to the throne of England.

In Norway, King Harald Sigurdsson—Harald Hard-Ruler (*harðráði*)—was the archetypal Viking still, schooled in the rough disciplines of Byzantine raids and the merciless power-politics of Scandinavia. He had been king of Norway for nearly twenty turbulent years when he decided to revive the lapsed dynastic claim to England.

In the late summer of 1066, Harald Hard-Ruler set sail across the North Sea with an invasion armada of more than three hundred ships, intent on the crowning achievement of his Viking career. On September 20 he landed his army of some nine thousand men in Yorkshire, brushing aside what little local opposition there was.

In London, Harold Godwinsson had been waiting to hear who would be the first to invade, the Northmen or the Normans. When the news of the landing in Yorkshire reached him, he force-marched his army north for nearly two hundred miles and fell upon Harald Hard-Ruler at Stamford Bridge.

For once the old Viking was taken by surprise. By nightfall most of the Norwegian army had been wiped out, and Harald Hard-Ruler himself lay dead. Nineteen days later, Harold of England met his own death on the south coast at the Battle of Hastings trying to beat off a second invasion. Duke William of Normandy took the vacant throne, and England from then on was committed not to Scandinavia but to the continent. For England, the Battle of Stamford Bridge was to all intents and purposes the end of the Viking Age.

2

Scotland: the Earldom in the North

According to the early Icelandic historians, the Northern and Western Isles of Britain were taken over by the King of Norway late in the ninth century, to prevent them being used as bases by exiled Norwegian pirates:

> 'One summer King Harald Fine-Hair sailed west on a punitive expedition against the Vikings who raided the coasts of Norway all summer and wintered in Shetland or the Orkneys; for he was tired of their harrying. He subdued Shetland and the Orkneys and the Hebrides; he went all the way down to the Isle of Man and destroyed the settlement there. He fought many battles there, and extended his dominion further west than any King of Norway has done since then. One of those killed in battle was Ivar, the son of Earl Rögnvald of Möre; so when King Harald set sail for Norway, he gave Earl Rögnvald the Orkneys and Shetland as compensation for the loss of his son. Earl Rögnvald in turn handed over both countries to his brother Sigurd, who was King Harald's prow-man; King Harald bestowed on him the title of Earl, and Sigurd stayed behind in the west when King Harald returned to Norway.'
> (*Orkneyinga Saga*, Chapter 4)

Orkneyinga Saga (The Saga of the Orkneymen) is the main documentary source for the history of the Northern Isles in Viking times. It was written in Iceland around 1200 AD, but as history it must be treated with great caution. It is *saga*-history: the dynastic story of the Norse earls of Orkney, a vivid narrative pageant of clashing personalities and dramatic events. These Norse earls ruled a miniature empire of the north; from their headquarters in Orkney they controlled Shetland, the Hebrides, and extensive areas of the north and west of mainland Scotland.

The Icelandic saga-historians tended to relate the history of all the North Sea countries to the political developments in Norway that led to the settlement of Iceland late in the ninth century—the rise to power of King Harald Fine-Hair (see Chapter 6). But it is now clear from the evidence of archaeology that the Norwegian take-over of the Northern Isles had begun much earlier—before the start of the ninth century, at least three generations before King Harald Fine-Hair came to power in Norway.

The Northern Isles were never an independent nation, like Iceland, but they were more than merely a Norwegian colony. At the height of its power, from the mid-ninth to the mid-twelfth centuries, the Orkney earldom formed the political focus of a semi-independent Norse state that sat astride the trade-routes of the north. Some of the stronger earls could even challenge the throne of Norway, and get away with it for a time. The Orkneys were a prosperous agricultural community, exporting hides, fish, whale oil, and the homespun cloth (*vaðmál*) that was the staple of northern commerce. On top of this came wealth derived from tribute from neighbours, from trade and from occasional raiding.

The effect of the Viking occupation was more pronounced and lasting in Shetland and the Orkneys than anywhere else in Scotland. Practically all the place-names there are Norse in origin, and so is the whole cultural background. In Shetland a Norse dialect called Norn was spoken until the nineteenth century, and the northern islanders of today still feel a distinct affinity with Norway. So thoroughly was Scotland orientated on Orkney that to this day the northernmost county of the mainland is called Sutherland—the southland.

Before the first Norwegians arrived, some time late in the eighth century, the Northern Isles had been inhabited by a native people known as the Picts. It is rather a vague term, first applied by the Romans to the fierce northern natives they failed to subdue in Scotland (*Picti*, 'the painted ones'), and used also by the Norsemen (*Péttar*). Very little is known about their origins. They were simply the people who were there when the Vikings arrived.

In the Northern Isles the Viking take-over was so complete that the Picts just vanished from the history of the north. Some scholars have thought, because of this, that there had never been any Picts in the Orkneys—that the islands had been empty when the Norsemen arrived. Others believed they were exterminated by the invaders.

Three small silver bowls were found packed together in the buried hoard in St Ninian's Isle in Shetland.

This latter deduction seemed to be confirmed by the discovery in 1958 of a hoard of buried silver plate under the floor of the remains of a medieval church on St Ninian's Isle, just off the west coast of Shetland. It was a unique collection of twenty-eight pieces of native silverwork from the Dark Ages. All the objects, including a superb silver hanging-bowl, had been hastily crammed into a larchwood box bound with copper, and this box had then been buried upside down under a slab of stone lightly incised with a cross. Professor David Wilson of University College, London, now thinks that the hoard was the secular plate of a local chief hidden in a church in the face of a Viking raid at the end of the eighth century; but at the time the excavator, Professor Andrew O'Dell of the Geography Department of Aberdeen University, believed that the objects were precious church plate. In his report he envisaged a dramatic scene of panic and confusion in the darkness of the little church, as the priests hid away their treasures at the approach of Viking raiders.

On the other hand, the earliest levels of Norse occupation excavated in the Northern Isles so far have yielded almost no traces of weapons, which suggests that the first Norse colonists were men of peace. And a recent excavation at the Point of Buckquoy, on the north-west coast of the main island of the Orkneys, indicates that the Viking take-over involved peaceful assimilation rather than violent conquest.

At Buckquoy in 1970 and 1971 Dr Anna Ritchie of Edinburgh University excavated a low mound some sixty feet long, half of which had already been destroyed by coastal erosion. The site

44

contained evidence of four major periods of human occupation: the first two Pictish and the last two Norse, spanning a period of three hundred years from the seventh to the tenth centuries. The most extraordinary feature of this much-used site was that the later Pictish house was practically a Norse long-house, a most elaborate building with curved walls constructed with considerable architectural skill; it had carefully made drystone walls and a long-fire down the middle of the main room in which peat had been burned.

The Norse house that was built almost on top of it early in the ninth century, some fifty years later, contained no distinctly Norse artefacts. There were several bone pins and combs whose decoration was familiar from Pictish sites, and the pottery was Pictish as well. Apart from the architectural style of the building, the only objects of arguably Norse origin were three stone gaming-boards incised with

Slab-lined grave near the ruins of early Pictish and Viking houses at Buckquoy.

45

This incised stone slab from Buckquoy had been used to play a game like draughts or fox-and-geese. It measures about eight inches across.

criss-cross lines like a chessboard, on which some sort of battle-game seems to have been played.

The inference seems to be that the early settlers at Buckquoy simply took over and assimilated the native culture they found there, and presumably the natives as well, since it was not too alien to them. They borrowed Pictish customs, household utensils, and art-forms, and made them their own. They built their houses on the same sites, and farmed in much the same way, growing oats and bere (a type of barley), rearing sheep and cattle, and collecting shellfish from the shore. The Buckquoy excavation demonstrated, for the first time, a startling degree of cultural admixture between the new settlers and a sophisticated native population.

On the southern tip of Shetland, the cliffs of Sumburgh Head rear abruptly to a height of about 200 feet. Behind this forbidding promontory the ground sinks to a stretch of sandy dunes and rocky foreshore cradling the shelving beach of the West Voe of Sumburgh. This sheltered bay is a natural harbour, ideal for drawing up boats.

The bay is dominated by the ruins of a baronial medieval building that Sir Walter Scott had romantically named Jarlshof (Earl's Temple) in his novel *The Pirate*; he had wrongly associated it with the Norsemen, but the name was to prove prophetic, for archaeology has revealed at Jarlshof a remarkable evolving complex of Norse houses extending back to the early period of the Viking occupation.

46

In 1897 a series of violent storms eroded the promontory near the head of the bay on which Jarlshof stands, exposing large stone walls that had been buried under the sands. Gradually it became clear that the sand concealed an archaeological site of great importance.

There was some desultory excavation at the beginning of this century, but it was not until the 1930s that the site began to be systematically investigated under Dr A. O. Curle. He started uncovering layer upon layer of settlements dating back to well before 1000 BC. These settlements had been abandoned in succession as sand drifted in from the nearby dunes, covering first the oval stone-built huts of the earliest farmers, then the substantial Bronze Age village that later arrivals built on top of them, then the massive stone *broch* (round tower) that newcomers built in the first century AD, followed by another major settlement of 'wheel-houses' built by the people generically known as Picts. These Pictish farmers lived on there for about six or seven centuries—until the Viking settlers arrived at the end of the eighth century.

It was Dr Curle, in fact, who excavated at Jarlshof the first Viking homestead to be positively identified anywhere in the British Isles. That was in 1934. But it was to be another twenty years before the whole of the three-acre site at Jarlshof was cleared, by J. R. C. Hamilton, and the full story of the first Viking colonists there emerged.

It was basically a single farm that had been adapted and enlarged by succeeding generations. The first farmhouse, dated to the first half of the ninth century, was a rectangular long-house of characteristic Scandinavian form, built of stone with alternating courses of turves. It measured about sixty-five feet by twenty feet, and was divided into two rooms—a long living-room and a smaller kitchen. The living-room had a long-fire down the centre of the room (a bed of red ash was discovered still in place), and down both sides of the room there had once been a raised dais. This was where the tables were set up for meals, and where members of the household slept at night.

Not far from this parent house was a number of outbuildings, including a byre, a smithy, and a small square building originally thought to have been a small family temple, but now interpreted as a bath-house in which water would be thrown onto heated stones to make steam for a sauna bath.

These first Shetland Vikings were farmers rather than fishermen. Some six hundred finds were made in the middens and the buildings themselves, and all the evidence suggested that the settlers relied on agriculture and husbandry for their subsistence: there were only

five stone sinkers for fishing-lines found at this layer, although it seems that fishing was later to become a major occupation for their descendants. In the middens were found some small bone pieces, or gags, that were used to stop lambs from suckling their mothers so that the ewes' milk could be used for human consumption. And there were many stone loom-weights for the upright looms on which homespun cloth was woven for both domestic use and export.

Perhaps the most interesting finds, however, were those which showed the Norsemen and their boats as drawn by themselves. On the floor of the first farmhouse, Dr Curle found in 1934 a thin tablet of slate on which one of the settlers had scratched a diagram of a Viking longship with a high prow and stern, a steering paddle on the starboard side, and a single mast. In 1951, excavation of the house-midden by Hamilton produced several more of these incised slates depicting a series of boats and animals, and a dragon-headed prow. There were also two memorable portraits: one of a young man (perhaps the artist himself?), curly-haired and bearded, wearing a tunic with a high collar, and the other of an older man, also bearded, with a sharp nose. There is nothing warlike about their appearance; and indeed only three fragments of weapons were found at the earliest levels of Norse occupation.

Many of the other finds reflected a high standard of artistry: there were innumerable examples of carved work, including finely-decorated bone combs, and several bone pins that had been shaped with great skill with animal-heads or axe-heads or thistle-heads.

As time went by, the Jarlshof settlement expanded as the family became more prosperous. Over the next four hundred years out-buildings were added, the original farmhouse was extended and then completely rebuilt. It was a place of peace, where children could play in safety: a tiny toy quern was found, and down by the seashore archaeologists found a semi-circle of small water-worn pebbles that had been laid out as part of a children's game.

Orkneyinga Saga offers a charming glimpse of this quiet and prosperous little community in the middle of the twelfth century. In the year 1148, Earl Rögnvald Kali of Orkney (the earl who founded St Magnus Cathedral in Kirkwall) was shipwrecked on Shetland on his way home from Norway. He was an affable and genial man with a rare sense of humour and a talent for making extempore verses, and *Orkneyinga Saga* relates that he stayed in Shetland all summer. One day he went down to Sumburgh disguised as a peasant, wearing a white cowl to conceal his face. At Sumburgh he met an old crofter-

The excavated remains of one of the Viking houses and paths at Jarlshof in Shetland.

fisherman who was disconsolate over the fact that his partner had failed to turn up for the day's fishing; so the Earl volunteered to take the missing man's place at the oars. They rowed out into the fierce currents off Sumburgh Head, where the old man nearly died of fright at the Earl's reckless seamanship; but the Earl managed to row the boat out of the tide-race, and they returned to Jarlshof with a good catch. When they beached the boat and started to divide the catch in the traditional way (one third for the boat, one third for each of the fishermen), a crowd of villagers gathered on the shore. The disguised Earl, as became a man who was later to be hailed as a saint, promptly handed his share over to the poor. Then, as he was leaving, he slipped on the wet bank of the beach and slid back to the bottom in a most undignified way. One of the women in the crowd burst out laughing, and soon they were all roaring with laughter at the Earl's discomfiture. Earl Rögnvald Kali showed no sign of being offended; he merely tossed off an impromptu stanza, just enough to let the onlookers know who he really was:

Portraits of a young
man and an old man
at Jarlshof

> 'The silken-clad lady
> Laughs at my clothing,
> She laughs more loudly
> Than befits a maiden.
> None knows an Earl
> In fisherman's guise,
> Yet Earl earlier
> Drew boat from the billows.'

With that the Earl went on his way, leaving the crowd suitably abashed.

Some time late in the thirteenth century the settlement at Jarlshof seems to have declined, despite the excellent fishing on its doorstep. No one knows why. Perhaps the drifting sand became too much to cope with and it was abandoned, to lie buried and forgotten until its rediscovery this century.

Considering the extent and duration of the Norse occupation of northern Scotland, it is remarkable that only nine Viking settlements have been identified and properly excavated—four in the Orkneys, two in Shetland, two in the Hebrides, and one in Caithness. Nor have Viking graves been found in any great numbers, either on the mainland or in the islands. This is probably due to the influence of Christianity on the pagan burial customs of the Norwegian incomers. *Orkneyinga Saga* records a dramatic meeting between Earl Sigurd

An artist's impression of what the settlement at Jarlshof looked like at the peak of its prosperity

the Stout of Orkney and King Olaf Tryggvason of Norway shortly before Olaf seized the throne of Norway in 995. Olaf Tryggvason, newly baptised in the Scilly Isles and fierce with evangelistic fervour, came to Orkney with a fleet of five ships and encountered Earl Sigurd, who had only three. Olaf called Sigurd onto his ship and said to him, 'I want you and all those who serve you to be baptised, or else you shall die here on the spot and I shall put all the islands to the sword and the fire.' Earl Sigurd was outnumbered, and was reluctant to die for his faith under such circumstances. Instead he agreed to become baptised and, according to *Orkneyinga Saga*, that was how all the Orkneys were converted to Christianity.

The archaeological evidence, however, suggests that the Christianisation of the Norsemen was a gradual process that seems to have started very early on. In 1882, a local antiquary found a remarkable boat-burial in Kiloran Bay on the island of Colonsay, in the Inner Hebrides, which demonstrated this early fusing of religions.

The grave itself was bounded by an unusual rectangular enclosure, fifteen feet long by ten feet broad, formed by rough slabs of stone. At one end of it lay the remains of the skeleton of a short, powerfully-built man lying crouched on his left side. He had been buried in a boat which had originally filled the enclosure: about a hundred and thirty iron rivets with round heads and square rivet-plates were found scattered over the whole area, and some of them had traces of wood still adhering to them. The dead man's horse had been buried with him, at the other end of the boat, and one of the horse's hind legs had been cut off just before the burial.

He had evidently been a person of some standing. He had been buried with a full complement of weapons—a double-edged iron sword, an axe, spear, arrows, knives, and shield. There were various ornaments, including a bronze ring-headed pin. He also seems to have been a trader; by his knees were found a pair of bronze scales, a balance-beam from which to hang them, and seven lead weights which had been decorated with bronze plates and enamel ornamentation. Two Anglo-Saxon coins found in the grave indicated that the burial had taken place in the second half of the ninth century—yet two of the stone slabs of the enclosure had been roughly incised with a Christian cross. It meant that a full century before Earl Sigurd the Stout and all the Orkneys were forcibly converted, according to *Orkneyinga Saga*, a Viking warrior-merchant in the Inner Hebrides was being buried in high pagan style, but with Christian overtones.

Despite occasional finds of this nature, the number of excavated settlement sites in Scotland is still so small that archaeologists are chary of drawing firm conclusions about the true nature of the Norse colonisation. Even so, sufficient has been found to corroborate the general picture given by *Orkneyinga Saga* of a dynamic and prosperous community that lived on agriculture, commerce, and occasional raiding to supplement the family income.

In March 1858 one of the finest treasure-hoards ever found in Britain was unearthed by a boy who was out hunting rabbits near the

An oval bronze brooch, 4½ inches by 2¾ inches, from the grave of a wealthy woman at Westness in the Orkneys.

beach of Skaill Bay, on the west side of the mainland of Orkney. The rabbit he was chasing bolted down a hole, and at the mouth of the burrow the boy found a few fragments of silver that the rabbits had uncovered. A treasure hunt ensued; eager neighbours scrabbling into the burrow found no fewer than ninety silver objects weighing about sixteen pounds. These were all later recovered for the Exchequer as treasure-trove and are now in the National Museum of Antiquities in Edinburgh—great penannular brooches, neck-rings, arm-rings, and ingots of silver. A large number of English and Arabic coins proved that the hoard had been deposited in the second half of the tenth century.

In 1963, archaeologists found an immensely rich Viking grave at Westness on the Orkney island of Rousay. It was the grave of a lady of high rank who died in the middle of the ninth century and was buried with her personal treasures and ornaments, including two large bronze shoulder-brooches superbly ornamented, and a magnificent long-pinned silver gilt cloak-pin of native make.

One of the most important Norse sites in the Northern Isles is on the Brough of Birsay, a small tidal islet, barely half a mile across, that lies off the north-west point of the mainland of Orkney, facing Buckquoy. Access on foot is only possible at low tide, over difficult rocks, and the Brough itself is a natural fortress. There was a Christian monastery there in early times, and it did not take the Vikings long to recognise its strategic advantages. As early as the ninth century, it seems, a Norse farmstead was built, consisting of at least two long-houses; but the incomers took care not to encroach on the Pictish church that stood there already—a broken Pictish headstone has survived at the head of a triple grave, incised with Pictish symbols and depicting three richly-clad figures, perhaps three army officers, who died in the eighth century. This careful respect for sacred places was not unusual in the Viking Age, but may come as a surprise to those nurtured on the schoolboy myth of barbarous Viking savagery.

In time, this farmstead on Birsay developed into a highly complex establishment which included the palace of one of the most formidable of Orkney's Norse earls, Thorfinn the Mighty, and the palace and cathedral of the Bishop of Orkney. In the eleventh century, Birsay was to all intents and purposes the capital of Orkney.

At the centre of this complex is the ruin of an eleventh-century Norse church built on top of the pre-existing Pictish church. It was made of split flagstone, with a rectangular nave and a square choir with a circular apse. The choir and apse were paved with flagstones,

Remains of Viking buildings on the Brough of Birsay.

but the floor of the nave was of beaten earth, and in the centre of the floor was a grave covered by irregular flagstones containing the much-disturbed skeleton of a man who had been re-buried long after death. Beside the church were a number of rooms arranged round a courtyard which had a paved alley leading to a side-door into the church. This represents all that is left of the bishop's palace.

According to *Orkneyinga Saga*, the church on Birsay was built by Earl Thorfinn the Mighty in the middle of the eleventh century. He was an alarming man: huge in build, sharp-featured and ugly, black-haired and swarthy, beetle-browed and big-nosed. He was ambitious and ruthless and very shrewd; he ruled the Northern Isles for nearly fifty years, and by the time he died in about 1063 he was much the most powerful ruler in North Britain. Around the year 1048 he undertook a pilgrimage to Rome, a leisurely progress that took him en route to Norway, Denmark, and Germany. In Rome, the Pope granted him absolution for his sins. On his return, Earl

54

Thorfinn gave up warfare and devoted all his time to peaceful administration: 'He stayed constantly on Birsay, and there he built Christchurch, a splendid minster.' It was the first Norse bishopric in the Orkneys, and there can be little doubt that the ruined church on Birsay is that minster of Christchurch. The bishop's palace was added later.

On the slope below the cathedral complex, and reaching right to the edge of the cliff, lie the remains of what was once a great range of buildings. Erosion of the cliff has already destroyed much of the structure; but there are clear traces of a fine stone-built hall which had its own under-floor central heating—a system of ducts through which hot air from a fire-pit in an adjoining ante-chamber was circulated underneath the dais that ran down the side-walls. It is a particularly difficult site to interpret, but this very considerable establishment is believed to have been the palace of Earl Thorfinn himself, where the ageing leader spent his declining years administering his far-flung territories and seeking to do good works. He died not long before King Harald Hard-Ruler of Norway launched his ill-fated invasion of England in 1066; had Earl Thorfinn lived long enough to lend Harald his support, England might have had a Norwegian rather than a Norman king.

In England, the Viking Age ended abruptly with the defeat of King Harald Hard-Ruler in 1066. But in the Northern Isles it lasted for another century at least, to create the most impressive and enduring Norse monument of all: St Magnus Cathedral in Kirkwall, the capital of the Orkneys.

It was founded in 1137, when Kirkwall was still barely a village— a handsome, solid building of warm red sandstone that glows in the sunlight, dominating every view and vista.

It was founded by that Earl Rögnvald Kali who had so amused the peasants at Jarlshof. He was the nephew of the saintly Earl Magnus, who was executed by a rival to the earldom on the island of Egilsay in April 1115. In a shrewd political move, Rögnvald Kali vowed that if he ever succeeded in his own claim to the earldom, he would build in his martyred uncle's memory the most magnificent minster in Orkney. It is one of the few election promises in history that have been honoured to the letter.

Masons from Durham were imported to build it. A great shed was constructed over the area where the foundations were to be dug, and the whole site was covered with lime. On this lime the builders traced out all the dimensions with huge compasses, mapping out the pillars

St Magnus Cathedral in Kirkwall in the Orkneys.

and arches and walls, and then laid the foundation stones directly onto this full-scale blueprint. The first stage of building lasted seventeen years (it took three centuries to bring the Cathedral to its present complete state), and then Earl Rögnvald ran short of money; indeed, such an enormous project must have proved a severe strain on Orkney's economic resources. By then the apse, two bays of the choir and the two transepts were completed and roofed, and the Cathedral was in full use. The bishop had left Birsay for Kirkwall, and Earl Rögnvald had every reason to congratulate himself. The interior of the Cathedral was painted in brilliant colours, red, black and gold on a white background, and the walls themselves were hung with tapestries or the draped sails of Viking ships.

During restoration work on the fabric in 1919, a mason working on the south pillar of the choir noticed that some of the stones high up in the pillar were loose. When he prised them out, he found a small cavity inside containing a wooden casket, thirty inches long; inside the casket lay the bones and skull of a man.

When St Magnus was executed on the island of Egilsay, according to *Orkneyinga Saga*, he specifically asked that he should not be put to death by beheading, like a common slave, but that he should be killed by an axe-blow on the head, as befitted an aristocrat: 'With that he crossed himself and bowed his head to the stroke; and he was struck on the middle of the head with a single blow, and thus he passed from this world to the next.'

When the skeleton in the casket was examined, it turned out to be that of a well-built man, five feet seven and a half inches tall. And across the top of the skull there was a great wound that had been dealt by an axe. The relics of St Magnus had been found. Originally enshrined above the high altar, they must have been hidden away in that high place on the eve of the Reformation to safeguard them against the threat of sacrilege.

The building of St Magnus Cathedral in the twelfth century was the final flowering of the Viking Age in the north. From then on, Norse power gradually declined. After the Battle of Largs in 1263, the Hebrides were ceded to the Scottish crown. In the following century the dynastic line of Norse earls came to an end, and 'Scottified' earls took over. In 1468 the Orkneys were pledged to the Scottish crown for 50,000 florins of the Rhine as part of the dowry of the Danish princess Margaret on her marriage to King James III of Scotland (Norway and Denmark had become united under the Danish crown late in the fourteenth century); and in the following year, 1469, Shetland went the same way, pledged for a further 8,000 florins. Repeated attempts were made over the years to redeem the pledges, but by now the Northern Isles were irrevocably Scottish, and there could be no turning the clock back to the Golden Age of the Viking earls.

3

The Isle of Man: Kingdom in Microcosm

Much the smallest of the countries in the path of the Viking surge westwards was the Isle of Man. It is only 227 square miles in area, and lies in the middle of the Irish Sea. Today it is an independent sovereign country under the British crown, yet it has preserved unbroken more of the traditional Viking elements than any other former Viking colony in the British Isles. Geographically it occupies a pivotal position, very nearly equidistant from Ireland, Scotland, England and Wales, all of which can be clearly seen from the top of Snaefell, the highest point of the island (2,034 feet).

Down on the plains to the south-west is Tynwald Hill. The name Tynwald is Norse in origin (*Thingvöllur*) and means literally Parliament Plain. This is believed to have been the site of the Viking Assembly (*Thing*) which met in the open air every summer to help the king and local chieftains legislate and administer justice; and every summer still, on Old Midsummer Day (5 July), the modern Parliament, which is still called the Tynwald, meets there for an open-air ceremony to promulgate the laws that have been passed during the year. Dingwall in the north of Scotland and Tingwall in Shetland echo a similar past as a place of Viking assembly, but no trace of the original institution survives as it does in Man.

No one knows precisely when the first Viking assembly was held at Tynwald, or even when the first Vikings arrived on Man. The Irish annals record a Viking raid in 798 on an island called Inis Patraic, which has been identified with St Patrick's Isle, a tiny islet off the old fishing port of Peel, about two miles from Tynwald Hill, but most scholars no longer accept this identification. It seems clear from the archaeological evidence, however, that the Vikings began to colonise Man in the ninth century: a large boat-burial at Balladoole in the south of the island, containing a variety of personal possessions of Scandinavian, continental and Irish origin, is dated 850–900. Another boat-burial, at Knoc y Doonee in the north of the island, suggests a similar date; it was a large mound containing the decayed remains of a thirty-foot boat in which a warrior had been buried with all his weapons and tools and his horse.

Some forty Viking graves have been excavated on the island, and they suggest that the Vikings were quick to adopt Christianity, or some aspects of it at least, from the Irish Celts who were on the island when they arrived. They made a habit of burying their dead in Christian churchyards—but the dead man's sword was placed in the grave as well. Throughout the tenth century, paganism and Christianity became intermingled in sometimes bizarre ways.

One grave, however, offers evidence of a practice that was purely pagan—human sacrifice. It was a burial mound at Ballateare in the north of the island, and it was excavated by Professor Gerhard Bersu in 1946. In it a man had been buried in a coffin with all his weapons, which seem to have been deliberately broken before the interment—either to disappoint grave robbers, or to render the weapons useless

An Iron Age hill fort, later used as a Celtic cemetery, at Balladoole. At the bottom left, outlined by blocks of stone in the shape of a boat, is a Viking burial.

in case the dead man tried to haunt the living. When the coffin had been lowered into the grave a circular mound of soil was heaped up over it. But before the mound was completed, another body was laid on it. This was the body of a young woman in her twenties, lying face

Part of a carved stone cross from Kirk Andreas shows Óðin attacked by the wolf Fenrir.

downwards with her arms raised above her head. At the top of her skull there was a hole made by a blow from a heavy instrument.

There seems little doubt that this was the skeleton of a slave-girl, or perhaps even the dead man's wife, who had been sacrificed to accompany him to the other world. It is known from documentary sources that Viking slave-girls were sometimes sacrificed in this way: the Arab writer Ibn Fadlan wrote an account of his visit to Bulgar in Russia in 922, which contains a detailed description of the funeral of a Viking chieftain in the east and the gruesome ceremonies that accompanied the ritual death of the wretched girl chosen for the privilege of accompanying her master. Graves have been found in Scandinavia that seem to represent sacrificial funerals of this kind, including the royal ship-burial at Oseberg in Norway, but the Ballateare burial is the only known example yet found in the British Isles.

The other major source of information about the Viking period in Man is the magnificent collection of carved stone crosses. They are to be found in churchyards all over the island, and casts of them all can be seen in the Manx National Museum in the island's capital, Douglas. These, too, show a distinctive mixture of Norse and Celtic culture and religion.

Unusually, we know the name of the sculptor who carved many of the earliest of these stones. A stone at Kirk Michael in the north-west of Man has an inscription that says it was erected by Melbrigði, son of Aðakan the Smith, 'but Gaut made this and all in Man'.

From another cross at Kirk Andreas we learn that his full name was Gaut Björnsson, and that he lived at Kuli, possibly the farm of Cooill or Cooley in the parish of Michael, or else the Scottish island of Coll. His work is dated to the period 930–50, and he seems to have been the first Scandinavian to introduce and adapt Celtic crosses in Man. His grave-slabs were rectangular blocks of stone on which a typical wheel-headed Celtic cross was incised in low relief. The patterns he applied were relatively simple interlaced bands in a Norwegian ring-chain motif. It seems that he learned his craft in the north-east of England, where patterns of this kind have been noted; and he may well have been a Viking refugee from Cumberland, say, after the major Norse defeat at the Battle of Brunanburh in 937.

Later stone slabs represent an even more vivid blend of cultures. A stone at Kirk Braddan was raised by a Viking called Thorleif for a son with the very Celtic name of Fiacc. The ornamentation is directly derived from the so-called Mammen style with its ribbon-shaped animals, and suggests that the Manx Vikings remained in contact with Norway itself as well as the Norse areas of Ireland and northern England.

Some of the stones carry scenes that represent a total fusion of pagan and Christian ideas and myths. The Thór Stone from Bride depicts a Christian cross with the chief Norse god Óðin standing below it, while at the head of the shaft two dwarfs are holding up the firmament. On the other side stands a bearded Thór, the thunder-god, and one of the panels depicts one of the most celebrated incidents in Norse mythology—the fishing expedition when Thór tried to catch the terrible World Serpent that lay coiled around the earth. Thór hooked the serpent, using a sheep as bait, but his companion in the boat took fright and cut the line.

An even later cross from Kirk Andreas shows Óðin naked with a raven on his shoulder. His leg is gripped in the jaws of the ferocious wolf Fenrir who in Norse mythology was destined to devour Óðin in the Last Battle, the *Ragnarok*, when the old gods met their doom.

Three handsome picture stones, at Jurby, Maughold and Malew, show scenes from the legend of Sigurd the Dragon-Slayer, the hero who slew the dragon Fáfnir to rescue the Treasure of the Nibelungs.

Norse mythology, Norse art, Norse inscriptions, Norse place-names like Dalby and Snaefell, Norse institutions like Tynwald—all these are indications of the time when the Isle of Man was a Viking kingdom in microcosm; they mirror to this day a Viking past more clearly, perhaps, than anywhere else in the British Isles. Man remained a Viking possession until 1266; its kings, descended from the Icelandic-born Godred Crovan, all more or less owed allegiance to the kings of Norway, who also appointed the lord bishops whose diocese embraced both Man and the Hebrides. The bishopric is known to this day as 'Sodor and Man', from the Norse name for the Hebrides (*Suðreyjar*, meaning 'South Islands').

The last Scandinavian king of Man was Magnus (1252–66), who agreed to accept the overlordship of King Alexander III of Scotland. After the attachment of the Isle of Man to Scotland, the lordship of Man changed hands frequently as English sovereigns laid claim to the island and sold or awarded the 'kingship' to their own courtiers. Finally, in 1828, the British government bought the lordship on behalf of the Crown for £417,000. But Man did not lose its unique position as a sovereign kingdom within the British Isles, with its own home parliament, ruled now by a 'Lord of Mann' who happens also to be the monarch of Great Britain.

A carved stone cross from Kirk Braddan has a runic inscription up the side. The first letters spell '*þorleifr*' (Thorleif).

4

Ireland:
Saints and Sinners

'In a word, although there were an hundred hard-steeled iron heads on one neck, and an hundred sharp, ready, never-rusting brazen tongues in every head, and an hundred garrulous, loud, unceasing voices from every tongue, they could not recount or narrate or enumerate or tell what all the people of Ireland suffered in common, both men and women, laymen and priests, old and young, noble and ignoble, of hardship and injury and oppression in every house from these ruthless, wrathful, foreign, purely pagan people.'

Thus the writer of *The War of the Irish with the Foreigners* (*Cogadh Gaedhel re Gallaibh*) described the miseries that the Vikings are alleged to have inflicted on Ireland. It is rhetoric, and preposterous rhetoric at that. Moreover, it was written in the twelfth century, at least 350 years after the Viking raids began, and for a specifically nationalistic purpose. And yet until very recently, this was the generally accepted picture of what the Vikings did to the Irish.

It is now beginning to be recognised that *The War of the Irish with the Foreigners* has little historical basis. It was written to glorify the deeds of the celebrated Irish king Brian Boru, the first man to impose royal authority over the whole of Ireland, who fell at the Battle of Clontarf in the year 1014. In much the same way as the chronicler Geoffrey of Monmouth in the twelfth century (*The History of the Kings of Britain*) elevated an obscure sixth-century English war-leader called Arthur to the status of a great Christian emperor for nationalistic reasons, so the Irish author made Brian Boru into a peerless Christian hero defending his native land against the Viking hordes; and in the course of this panegyric, he felt impelled to dramatise the ferocity and cruelty of the Vikings, to make Brian Boru's achievements all the more noteworthy. The author was inventing for Ireland a stirring image of national resistance to the invaders, all the more heroic for being fought against great odds.

Following his example, historians have tended to create a sharp distinction between the centuries of 'Viking Terror' and the 'Age of Saints' that preceded them. Ireland at this time was one of the leading centres of Christianity in Europe. From its beginnings in the fifth century, the Irish Church had reached a peak of wealth and learning and literature. Her missionaries were all over Europe. Her artwork, as typified by the magnificent Ardagh Chalice of the early eighth century, was unsurpassed. There were no mercantile towns or trade-centres in Ireland at this time, although the great monastic centres like Armagh and Clonmacnoise and Clonfert were practically ecclesiastical capitals in their own right.

All this glory the Vikings were said to have destroyed. The first recorded Viking raid on Ireland took place in the year 795, with an attack on the island of Reachrainn, which is usually identified with the island of Lambay off the east coast near Dublin, but is more likely to have been Rathlin Island, five miles off the north-east corner of Ireland; for the first Vikings came prowling down the west coast of Scotland from the Orkneys and the Hebrides. From then on, according to the Irish chroniclers, there was no respite:

> 'The sea spewed forth floods of foreigners over Erin, so that no harbour, no landing-place, no stronghold, no fortress, no fastness might be found, but it was submerged by waves of Vikings and pirates ... so that they made spoil-land and sword-land and conquered-land of her, throughout her breadth and generally; and they ravaged her chieftainries and her privileged churches and her sanctuaries; and they rent her shrines and her reliquaries and her books.'

In actual fact, however, the 'Age of Saints' was not quite the peaceful era it has been painted. Dr A. T. Lucas, Director of the National Museum of Ireland, has pointed out that prior to that first Norse raid in 795, the Irish annals record the burning of monasteries on at least thirty occasions—by the Irish themselves: 'We are left with the indelible impression that plundering or burning was a normal hazard of a church or monastery in ancient and medieval Ireland.' Ireland was a turmoil of squabbling tribes and petty kings, and the monasteries of enemy tribes were legitimate targets. The

OPPOSITE
The Gokstad Ship in the Viking Ship Museum in Oslo.

abbots and monks themselves were frequently to be found in the thick of the fray, as in 807 when the monasteries of Cork and Clonfert fought a pitched battle which resulted in 'an innumerable slaughter of the ecclesiastical men and superiors of Cork'.

The monasteries were the main repositories of wealth in Ireland at this time; and not just in church treasures, but in provisions, livestock, and lands. Whenever there was famine, the Irish themselves would raid their monasteries for food. As Dr Lucas puts it, 'A short experience in the country would have taught even a freelance Viking band that a raid on an Irish monastery was a sound economic proposition.'

The early raids were sporadic and infrequent. In the first twenty-five years after 795, there are only twenty-six acts of Viking pillage recorded in the Irish annals, compared with eighty-seven acts of violence amongst the Irish themselves. Nor does bullion appear to have been the main aim of the Viking attacks on monastic settlements. A considerable amount of ecclesiastical metalwork has been found in Viking graves dating from the early years of the ninth century, but not everything that came to Norway from Ireland was loot from Viking raids. In the National Museum in Copenhagen there is a small Irish casket-shrine containing some relics. It used to be thought that a Viking had plundered it and taken it home to Norway as a jewellery-box, where a grateful wife or girl-friend had it incised with the inscription: 'Rannvaig owns this box'; but it is more likely to have been a gift from a Christian visitor to Norway.

The raids increased in intensity from 830 onwards. But there seems to have been no major attempt at colonisation until the year 840, when the annals record the arrival in Ireland of a formidable Norwegian sea-king said to be called Turgesius. He came with 'a great royal fleet', say the annalists, and made himself 'King of all the Foreigners in Erin'. He is alleged to have plundered Armagh Abbey and installed himself as Abbot there, pagan or no, and his wife Ota was said to have chanted heathen spells and oracles at the sacred altar of Clonmacnoise. Indeed, the author of *The War of the Irish with the Foreigners* accused Turgesius of trying to convert the whole of Ireland to Thór-worship, but this is so alien to the unfanatical Viking religious ethos that it cannot be taken seriously. Scholars no longer place much credence in Turgesius as a historical figure; and the modern Irish historian Donncha Ó Corráin now goes so far as to call the whole idea of a deliberate royal expedition from Norway at this time nonsense.

The reassembled Viking deep-sea trader, the *knörr*, in the Viking Ship Museum at Roskilde in Denmark. This is the only ship of its kind yet found.

This small Irish casket-shrine found in Norway was probably a visitor's gift rather than plunder from a Viking raid.

But there is no doubt that by the middle of the ninth century there were distinctly Viking communities resident in Ireland. There is ample archaeological evidence for this from the extensive Viking cemetery on the outskirts of Dublin at Kilmainham/Islandbridge. It was unearthed by accident in the middle of the last century during construction work on the Great Southern and Western Railway. It is the largest cemetery of its kind yet found outside Scandinavia, and although it was never systematically excavated, the finds that survived illustrate the preoccupations of this settlement of exiles.

There were some forty swords dating from the ninth century, many of them richly ornamented with silver patterns hammered into the hilt or pommel. Most of the swords were Norwegian, but others were Frankish, heavy and costly to acquire. There were more than a score of iron spear-heads and shield-bosses, some of them locally made, and two iron axe-heads, always a favourite Viking weapon. There were women's graves in this cemetery, too; they had been buried wearing their characteristic Norse tortoise-shaped (oval) brooches and necklaces of glass beads, or accompanied by their domestic accoutrements—wooden linen smoothers (calenders) and the stone spindle-whorls they used when making thread.

But the most significant graves were those of the craftsmen and merchants. Some of the dead men had been buried with their tools:

forge-tongs, pincers, hammers, shears, knives, sickles. Others had clearly been merchants, for a number of sets of folding bronze scales were found, their pans brightly tinned on the inside; and with them, a dozen handsomely-fashioned weights with lead cores, decorated with enamel and glass.

It is the evidence of these graves that points to the really important effect of the Vikings on Ireland. For they taught the Irish the business of trade, and helped add a mercantile side to Ireland's simple pastoral economy. The basic Irish vocabulary for commerce is borrowed from the Norse language—*margad* (*markaðr*, market), *pingin* (*peningr*, penny), and so on. The Irish also quickly adopted or adapted the superior Viking weapons to their own use; and they learned from the Vikings how to build and use sophisticated wooden ships to replace their own hide-covered *currachs*. A great number of

The hilt of one of the ninth-century swords found in the cemetery at Kilmainham/Islandbridge.

General view of the excavation of the Viking settlement at the High Street site in Dublin.

Irish words connected with ships and navigation are directly borrowed from the Norse: *accaire* (*akkeri*, anchor), *stiúr* (*stýri*, rudder), *scút* (*skúta*, small boat), and many others.

Most important of all, the Vikings founded the first trading-centres in Ireland, fortified sea-bases that became prosperous commercial towns. These towns were a completely new concept to the Irish, for the ecclesiastical centres like Armagh had never been interested in mercantile activity except on a strictly local basis. The Vikings brought Ireland into the mainstream of European trade. In 841, according to the annals, they established a *longphort* (ship enclosure) at the ford of the River Liffey, at a place known to the Irish as Dubh-Linn, the Black Pool. It was the start of the city of Dublin.

Across the street from the massive Gothic cathedral of Christ Church that dominates the heart of old Dublin, there stands a high fence of corrugated iron. The High Street traffic roars past, oblivious of the fence with its single locked door. It looks just like any other development site. Yet behind the corrugated iron there is a different world: the world of Viking Dublin.

Several feet below the surrounding street level, a group of men are engrossed in a delicate task. They are for the most part ex-navvies, yet they are working with the patient skill of archaeologists, trowelling, brushing, sifting through the soil an inch at a time. They are totally absorbed in their work. They are engaged in one of the most important Viking excavations outside Scandinavia: the recovery of a Viking town deep under the centre of a modern city.

It started in 1962, when Dr Breandán Ó Ríordáin of the National Museum of Ireland was given the opportunity of excavating a site on High Street that had been cleared for redevelopment. The story of the excavation can be read clearly on the walls of the great pit in which he and his helpers are still working.

The foundations of eighteenth-century buildings had been sunk to a depth of some eight feet, destroying all evidence of previous occupation down to that level. But beneath these cellars was a six-foot layer of compacted, dark-coloured debris that had accumulated from the ninth to the thirteenth centuries, barred and streaked with the detritus of successive layers of human occupation.

A bone comb from the High Street site.

This deep deposit looks not unlike peat, which had made earlier scholars think that Dublin had been built on a peat-bog when they sank trial bores into the ground; and it also has the remarkable preservative qualities of peat. Phosphates and tannins formed a protective coating of vivianite to prevent metal from corroding, and from this deep layer of debris have so far come more than 4,000 splendidly preserved items of archaeological and historical interest.

The bulldozers moved in first, to clear away the brick cellars. But the last six feet, right down to the underlying boulder clay, could only be tackled with trowels. Steadily the excavators worked their way down through the centuries. The first clear culture level they came to was the Norman period of the thirteenth century—a huge deposit of scrap leather which had obviously been the workshop of generations of leather-workers; it was four feet deep in some places. Underneath this deposit was found a coin of John, Lord of Ireland (later King John of England), dating from the last decade of the twelfth century; so the cobblers' shop was obviously later than that. But the cobblers were still working in the old Viking style; for the boots found in the pile were the same as those the archaeologists found at much deeper levels. Amongst the mass of discarded soles

A child's leather bootee from the thirteenth-century cobblers' shop.

and uppers they found children's shoes and bootees that have hardly changed at all in design to this day. It seems that when a Viking wore out his shoes, he did not trouble to have his soles patched: the sole was cut away and thrown out, and the uppers were used again to make another, slightly smaller, pair of shoes with new soles.

Below this level, Viking Dublin proper began to emerge with astonishing clarity. The Dublin of the eleventh century was a busy, thriving place. Here were streets and pavements of stone flags or scarred timber baulks like a crude frontier-town boardwalk. On either side of the streets were huddles of houses and workshops built in the post-and-wattle style—a series of upright dressed wooden posts with horizontal layers of wattles or rods woven between them, like basket-work. They were single-storey buildings, on average twenty-five feet by fifteen, and they were easy to erect, for the walls came in prefabricated units that were slotted neatly into the door-posts with their heavy oak jambs. Inside were stone-lined hearths, and all around were the rubbish-dumps that revealed just how well these Vikings had lived. Heaps of shells showed that they had eaten oysters, cockles, mussels and scallops. They had pork, beef, and mutton, as well as game delicacies like plover, snipe, woodcock and partridge. They had a large selection of fruit available, for the seeds of strawberries, apples, plums, cherries and blackberries were found. They had oats and wheat and barley in plenty, but the less well-off seem to have had to make do with the seeds of common weeds like goosefoot and pale persicaria. One find struck a familiar domestic note—a perfect, ossified, hen's egg.

There was also extensive evidence of a flourishing trade in wine. Everywhere there were pieces of broken pottery from Bristol and France, especially the handsome green-glazed pottery of Bordeaux. Fresh water was supplied through a long wooden conduit, marvellously preserved, made of hollowed tree-trunks with the top half acting as a lid.

One of the houses was occupied by craftsmen who specialised in making combs and others articles of bone, for it was full of hundreds of discarded or unfinished pieces. The combs were made chiefly from the antlers of red deer, and look very like modern combs. Pairs of sawn strips of bone formed the back plates, between which were riveted thin bone plates ready to be cut into teeth. Some of the combs had their own decorated comb-cases for protection when carried in Viking pockets. These comb-makers also made a variety of ornamented articles like gaming-pieces, bone whistles, and carved handles for knives. There was one particularly fine handle about five inches long, highly polished and faceted, with a dot-and-circle pattern incised on it; and there was a tiny chess piece in the form of a human bust, made from the tip of an antler-horn.

Woodworkers lived in another house, where they made circular lathe-turned bowls and platters, or large rectangular dishes hollowed from a single piece of wood and sometimes thriftily mended with metal stitches. Nearby lay the carved model of a toy Viking ship. A number of animal bones was found, mainly rib-bones and long bones with carved panels of decorative motifs. Some were just preliminary sketches, others were finished designs executed in full relief. They are known as 'trial pieces', and they were intended as patterns for casting in bronze the decorative panels used in metalwork of the period. One fine eleventh-century 'trial piece' shows how Viking and native Irish art-forms had fertilised each other, a sure sign of social and political assimilation: the Ringerike style with its interlaced foliate scrolls and trailing tendrils had been zoomorphised, and the tendrils had been given animal heads.

Metalwork was done in another of the houses. The craftsmen there left behind them baked clay crucibles in which to smelt bronze, and an ingot mould of steatite (soapstone) that had a matrix for casting Thór's Hammer symbols that were popular throughout the Viking world as good-luck amulets. The metalwork shows a close affinity with that of Scandinavia—decorated bronze needle-cases, brooch-

Bone trial piece from the High Street site

The remains of post-and-wattle walls of tenth-century buildings in the Winetavern Street site.

heads, bronze pins, and in particular a fine openwork gilt-bronze brooch decorated in the typical tenth-century Jellinge style with its fluid interlacing patterns.

Clearly, this area of the modern High Street had once been the craftsmen's quarter of Viking Dublin. And in this busy, pulsing area strange things happened. Two beautiful armlets of twisted gold strands were found, crushed as if in a fist, between thumb and forefinger. How had such treasures been mislaid? Or had they been hidden in time of war? Human skulls were also found, one of them with a great sword wound in it. And right at the bottom of the layer, sunk into the boulder clay itself, a shallow double grave, containing the cramped skeletons of a man and a woman.

But when had these people lived and died in Viking Dublin? It soon became clear that this was not the earliest part of the fortified township that had been established by the Vikings in 841. Right at the lowest level of occupation, just above the boulder clay, a coin was found that effectively dated the site; it was a coin of King Olaf Kvaran, one of the Norse kings who jockeyed for power in Ireland and Northumbria in the middle of the tenth century, and it was minted in 941—a full century after the chroniclers had recorded the foundation of the town.

So where had Dublin started? In 1969 the opportunity arose of excavating another cleared site alongside Winetavern Street, where the Corporation of Dublin proposes to build new civic offices. This street runs at a right angle to High Street, dropping quite steeply past the Cathedral of Christ Church towards the River Liffey to the north. The Winetavern Street site was considerably lower and further down the hill on which the High Street site and Christ Church Cathedral stand.

For three seasons Dr Ó Ríordáin interrupted his work in the High Street to excavate at the Winetavern Street site. Everywhere the same picture emerged—streets, post-and-wattle houses, and masses of artefacts. But one of the houses was significantly different: it was deeply sunken below the normal ground level, its floor about four feet below the street, and its walls had been formed of closely-set vertical timber planking. In it was found an Anglo-Saxon decorated strap-tag, which has been tentatively dated to the ninth century.

So here was an area of Viking Dublin that looked considerably earlier than the High Street site. It seems as if the original settlement started near the river, and then as it grew it expanded southwards up the hill, until it eventually formed the medieval town, enclosed by thick stone walls and measuring 700 yards by 300.

Dr Ó Ríordáin found a section of this medieval wall, which was

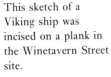

This sketch of a Viking ship was incised on a plank in the Winetavern Street site.

probably built in the twelfth century. But it was built on virgin
ground; there were no traces of Viking fortifications underneath it.
So despite the spectacular discoveries he has already made, he has
not yet found the very earliest part of Viking Dublin, the bank-and-
ditch fortification the Vikings would have thrown up to protect their
naval base on the Liffey. Only by excavating much nearer the banks
of the Liffey itself, he thinks, will he find evidence of the shape and
size of that first urban settlement in Ireland of 841.

However, he has already found enough to show that Dublin was
an exceptionally important town in Viking times. The Icelandic
sagas are full of references to Dublin as a good trade mart to visit. It
lay on the direct route from the north to France, and incidental
discoveries of fine fabrics woven with gold prove its pre-eminence
as a centre of commerce and wealth, and therefore of power.

Coin struck by
Sigtrygg Silk-Beard
in Dublin.

Other Viking towns whose names still echo their Scandinavian
origins played an important part in Irish politics—trading-centres
like Limerick, Waterford, Wicklow, and Wexford. They grew into
extensive Norse settlements, combining commerce and war, and
exercising intermittent influence on the bewildering turmoil of
skirmishes, attacks and counter-attacks that characterised Irish
history of this period.

But Dublin remained pre-eminent, the mercantile capital of the
country and the cockpit of Norse territorial ambitions in Ireland. A
succession of Norse chieftains installed themselves there as 'kings'
for longer or shorter periods. From Dublin they nurtured designs
on northern England and dreamed ambitiously of a united realm
of Northumbria and Ireland. But they never succeeded in subjugating the whole of Ireland under their rule, nor did any Norseman
seriously attempt to do so. It was amongst the local royal dynasties
of the Irish themselves that the political power-struggle was waged;
and it was not until the end of the tenth century that a man emerged
who almost succeeded in the impossible task of unifying all Ireland.
His name was Brian Boru.

Brian Boru became King of Munster in 976. Thirty years later,
after a series of ferocious struggles with rival kings, he was able to
claim authority over the whole country and style himself *imperator
Scottorum* (Emperor of the Irish). Later panegyrists were to cast him
in the role of an Alfred the Great, patron of the arts and literature,
founder of schools and churches, a reformer who created the first
national monarchy in defiance of the Vikings. The climax of his
career, according to this romantic image, was his final defeat of the

Vikings near Dublin at the Battle of Clontarf in 1014—a victory that cost him his own life.

This is an exaggeration. However, there were elements in this battle that appealed irresistibly to the popular imagination as far away as Scotland and Iceland. Clontarf, as Professor Gwyn Jones put it in his *History of the Vikings*, was too important to be left only to historians, so it was taken over by the legend-makers, who turned it into one of the most fateful and doom-laden battles in Viking history, the ultimate confrontation between the Irish and the Norse for the soul and sovereignty of Ireland.

Figurine, probably a chess piece, carved from the tip of an antler from the High Street site.

In fact the Battle of Clontarf was merely the conclusion of a revolt by the men of Leinster against the domination of Brian Boru. The Leinstermen sought allies amongst the Norse, as had happened so often before in Irish politics. To their aid came a motley collection of mercenaries—the Norsemen of Dublin under their king Sigtrygg Silk-Beard, Vikings from the Orkneys under Earl Sigurd the Stout, and Vikings from the Isle of Man under their leaders Brodir and Ospak. Battle was eventually joined outside the walls of Dublin on Good Friday, April 23, 1014. King Sigtrygg Silk-Beard prudently watched the fighting from behind the safety of Dublin's walls. By nightfall the Leinstermen and their Norse allies had been routed; Earl Sigurd of the Orkneys and Brodir of Man lay dead, along with 7,000 of their men. But in the hour of victory Brian Boru himself, High King of Ireland, was struck down and killed, as were his son and his grandson. And with that the legends began to proliferate, fed by the posthumously saintly heroism of the Irish king. Portents of doom, it was reported, had been seen on the night before the battle throughout the Norse world. Romantic interest was supplied by the role of a formidable queen, Gormflaith, mother of Sigtrygg Silk-Beard and former wife of Brian Boru and two other kings, who was promised to both Earl Sigurd and Brodir of Man as one of the prizes of victory, even though she must have been well over fifty.

Legend has made the Battle of Clontarf the climax of the Viking Age in Ireland, but it was by no means the end of it. King Sigtrygg Silk-Beard continued to rule Dublin for another twenty years. The Norsemen had already started minting their own coins in Dublin in the 990s, the first coins to be struck in Ireland, and for another 150 years they monopolised the trade in textiles and wine, and as before they profoundly influenced the development of the arts.

By the end of the tenth century the Ringerike style with its trailing tendrils had become part of the Irish craftsman's repertoire, exempli-

75

The magnificently
ornate head of the
tenth-century
'Crozier of the Abbots
of Clonmacnoise'.

fied in the handsome 'Crozier of the Abbots of Clonmacnoise'. This cross-fertilisation continued into the twelfth century. The Irish were the last to adopt and embellish the final phase of Viking art, the so-called Urnes style, named after the decoration of a small stave-church in the Sogn district of Norway. One of the finest pieces of ornamental metalwork ever made in Ireland was the outcome of this final flowering—the magnificent 'Cross of Cong', a processional cross some thirty inches high which was made as a reliquary for a fragment of the True Cross around the year 1123. Ribbon-like animals writhe all over the decorated panels, looping and biting, while the shaft of the cross itself is caught in the jaws of a large animal head.

But by now the Viking impetus was fading all over Europe. It was Duke William of Normandy, descendant of the Northmen, who

76

effectively brought England out of Scandinavia's orbit in 1066; and a century later it was the Normans who did the same for Ireland. William the Conqueror had never sought to subjugate Ireland by force of arms, as he did England and Wales, and throughout the eleventh and twelfth centuries Irish petty kings fought amongst themselves for control of Ireland. In the 1160s one defeated chieftain, Dermot MacMurrough Kavanagh, sought help from foreign mercenaries, just as his ancestors had done. This time the mercenaries were Norman soldiers from England, and within thirty years the incomers had overrun much of the country and consolidated their position in a series of wooden castles. From then on it was the Norman English, not the Vikings, who shaped Ireland's destiny.

The Cross of Cong.

5

The Faroes: Stepping-stones Northwards

Almost half-way between Shetland and Iceland, some two hundred miles out into the heaving Atlantic, lie the Faroes, an archipelago of precipitous islands that the Vikings named *Færeyjar* (Sheep Islands). The Vikings arrived there about 800, and found the islands occupied by flocks of sheep—and by Irish hermits.

For more than a century it had been the custom for Irish monks to seek solitude on remote islands where they could devote their lives exclusively to God. In their hide-covered *currachs* they launched themselves into daring and hazardous ocean journeys, and when they found an empty island they would settle there in tiny cells and spend the rest of their lives as hermits, with only a few sheep to keep themselves in food and clothing. They were *peregrini pro Christo*—wanderers for Christ; the Vikings called them *papar*—the Fathers.

The first *papar* seem to have reached the Faroes around 700. The Irish geographer Dicuil, who lived in France, wrote a treatise in 825 entitled *Liber de Menṣura Orbis Terrae* in which he described the earliest settlers:

'There are many other islands in the ocean to the north of Britain which can be reached from the northernmost British Isles in two days' and nights' direct sailing, with full sails and an undropping fair wind. A certain holy man informed me that in two summer days and the night between, sailing in a little boat of two thwarts, he came to land on one of them. Some of these islands are very small; nearly all of them are separated one from the other by

'The seas around the Faroes are perilous . . .' A stretch of forbidding coast at Mykines.

78

narrow sounds. On these islands hermits who have sailed from our Scotia [Ireland] have lived for roughly a hundred years. But, even as they have been constantly uninhabited since the world's beginning, so now because of Norse pirates they are empty of anchorites, but full of innumerable sheep and a great many different kinds of seafowl. I have never found these islands mentioned in the books of scholars.'

The 'books of scholars', in fact, have had very little to say about the Faroes. The main documentary source is an Icelandic saga written early in the thirteenth century, called *Færeyinga Saga* (the Saga of the Faroemen). Unlike *Orkneyinga Saga*, which was a dynastic history of the Earls of Orkney, *Færeyinga Saga* is by no means a history of the Faroes: it is a saga about the destiny of two men who competed for power and influence in the Faroes late in the tenth century—the peerless hero Sigmund Brestisson of Skúfey (Skúvoy), who was eventually killed by the shrewd and ruthless Thránd of Gata (Syðrugöta) who lived on the island of Austurey (modern Eysturoy). It is written in the classic saga tradition by an Icelander who does not seem to have known the Faroes personally, but whose account is based on oral traditions told to him by a Faroeman.

The saga records the earliest settlement:

'There was a man called Grím Kamban; he was the first man to settle in the Faroes. But in the days of King Harald Fine-Hair a great number of people fled [from Norway] because of his tyranny. Some settled in the Faroes and made their homes there, while others went to other uninhabited countries.'

The nickname Kamban seems to be cognate with Irish *camm*, meaning bent or crooked, so it is not unlikely that Grím came to the Faroes by way of Ireland or the Hebrides, where news of the practically uninhabited islands to the north would have been current. It seems likely that many of the early settlers were first- or second-generation Norsemen from the Scottish islands or Ireland, for they introduced a Celtic loan-word for the shielings high in the valleys where the dairy-work was done in summer: the word *ærgi*, found today in several Faroese place-names. Grím Kamban may have reached the Faroes as early as 820, although little is known of him from other sources; but the Icelandic historians associated the main bulk of the Viking settlement with the political pressure exerted by King Harald Fine-Hair of Norway from 870 onwards—the same pattern, indeed, as they proposed for the colonisation of Orkney.

OPPOSITE
Above The silver hanging-bowl from the treasure hoard found on St Ninian's Isle, Shetland.
Below Silver Viking neck-ring from the collection of ornaments found at Skaill Bay in the Orkneys.

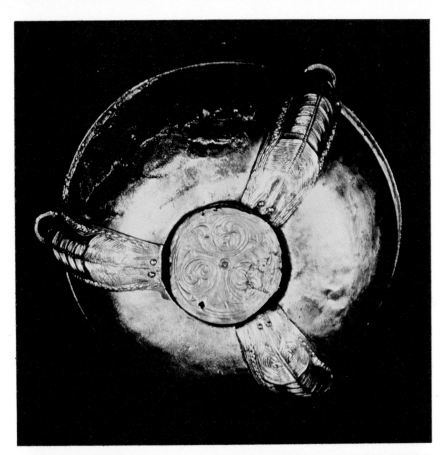

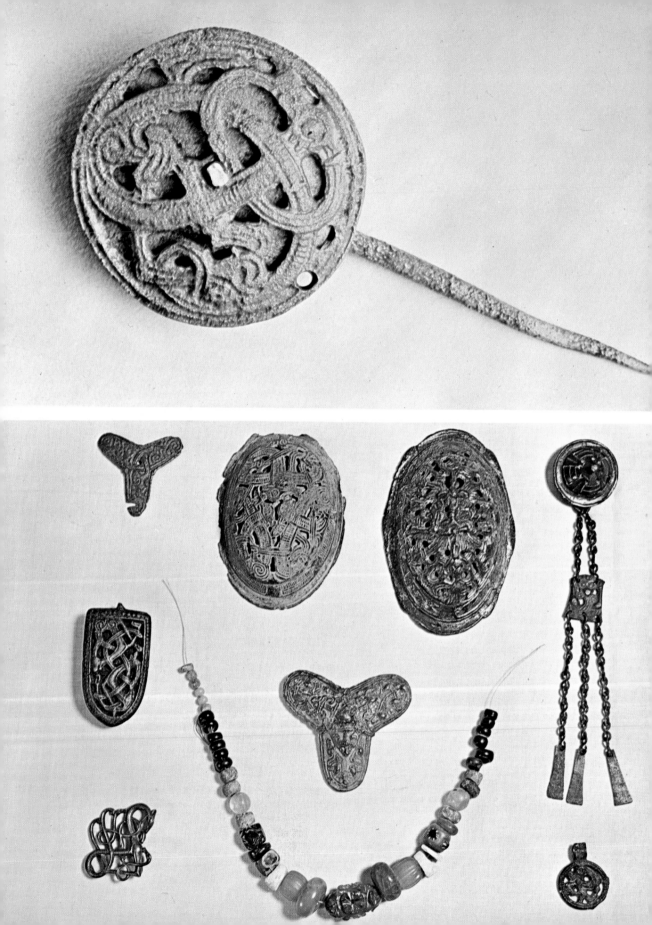

What little archaeological evidence has emerged so far in the Faroes neither proves nor disproves the early historical accounts. Little or no trace has yet been found of the *papar*, the Irish monks, apart from a hint of pre-Viking field-systems (on Mykines) and some inconclusive radiocarbon dates, but this is hardly surprising: they were not the men to build enduring monuments, their concern was all for the next world, not this one.

Only one Viking cemetery has been comprehensively excavated so far—a group of at least twelve graves in a dune of shifting sand at Tjörnuvík, the northernmost village on the island of Streymoy. One of them was surrounded by a stone frame shaped as a boat, as was common practice in Scandinavia, others had sides of stone slabs like a cist (chest). All the bodies had been buried with their heads in a northerly direction, whereas Christian burials are normally orientated east-west. The grave-goods were in poor condition. They included the remains of a knife, a buckle, and a boat-rivet, as well as a fairly well preserved ring-headed bronze pin with an ornamented head. This pin is of a North British type that has also been found in Iceland, and dates the grave to the tenth century; it is an indication of continuing communications between the Viking settlements in the Atlantic during the first centuries of colonisation.

A number of Viking Age houses have also been investigated. At Syðrugöta on Eysturoy the site of a large Viking farmhouse has been excavated, which it is naturally tempting to associate with Thránd of Gata in *Færeyinga Saga*. It had been greatly disturbed by later cultivation, and only one room remained discernible. It had a hearth in the middle of the floor, and a number of domestic utensils and personal objects were found, including beads, loom-weights, and flat-bottomed earthen vessels.

Another large Viking long-house has been excavated at Kvívík, on the western side of Streymoy. It was built so close to the shore that the sea has now eroded the lower end. The hall was fifty feet long and had curved double walls of stone infilled with earth. There was a long-fire down the centre of the hall. Several hundred objects were found in the hall, some of which had been imported, including steatite bowls and beads of amber and silver-foiled glass. There were also a pair of shoes of characteristic Norwegian type, and an enamelled bronze buckle-plate decorated with an animal motif. Beside the hall was a second building, a combined barn and cow-byre with accommodation for up to twelve head of cattle.

None of the finds suggests that the Faroes were ever as prosperous

Above Tenth-century gilt-bronze disc brooch found at the High Street site in Dublin. *Below* Viking Age ornaments found in Iceland.

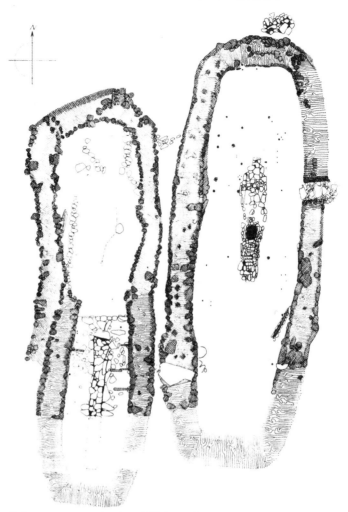

Ground plan of an early Norse farm at Kvívík. *Right* a typical long-house with a central fireplace; *left* a combined cow-byre and barn.

as the Orkneys were during Viking times. According to *Færeyinga Saga*, the Kings of Norway made efforts to extract tribute and taxes from the Faroes, although these efforts were usually foiled by the cunning of Thránd of Gata until the islands became a fief of the Norwegian crown in 1035. More than a hundred years later, however, the Faroese got revenge of a sort: a young man called Sverrir Sigmundsson left the islands and erupted into Norwegian politics like a whirlwind, seized the throne of Norway and ruled for twenty-five years (1177–1202). He proved to be one of Norway's more remarkable kings, and gave a great impetus to saga-writing by commissioning an Icelander to write a saga-biography of himself during his lifetime.

The Faroes can never have been easy to live in. As Earl Hakon of Norway says in *Færeyinga Saga*, 'The seas around the Faroes are perilous, with much surf, and longships cannot reach there.'

The economy was based on the sheep that still grazed the steep pastures on the island tops, on bird-fowling down the precipitous cliffs, on fishing (several stone sinkers for fishing-lines were found at Kvívík), and on the characteristic form of whaling still to be seen in the Faroes to this day—the driving ashore and killing of pilot-whales which enter the fjords in herds every August, there to be massacred in a blood-bath called the *grindedrab* (whale-killing).

Yet the Faroese established a thriving community, with their own local assembly or Thing at Tórshavn (Thór's Haven) which is now the capital of the Faroes. A hoard of nearly a hundred silver coins from all over Europe, which had been buried late in the eleventh century, suggests a measure of prosperity, at least for some. And late in the thirteenth century they built a fine stone cathedral dedicated to Saint Magnus of Orkney. It was never completed, apart from a chapel on the northern side, but it was nevertheless consecrated, and its magnificent roofless ruins are still to be seen at Kirkjubö, south of Tórshavn on the island of Streymoy; it has a reliquary said to contain relics of St Magnus.

The Viking colonisation of the Faroes was different in one important respect from their other enterprises further south: it was part of a policy of colonising new and uninhabited islands. The settlers were essentially farmers suffering from a growing land-hunger in their own countries, men who did not want to have to use force to dispossess a native population.

In this respect, the Faroes were stepping-stones to the most significant and enduring of the Viking enterprises in the Atlantic: the settlement of Iceland.

According to the early Icelandic historians, two at least of the first exploratory voyages to Iceland were launched from the Faroes in the middle of the ninth century. There is mention of an outlawed Norwegian Viking called Naddod; he was on his way home to the Faroes, where he had settled, when he was storm-driven to the east coast of Iceland. He found no sign of human habitation, and left as soon as he could. As he sailed away he saw snow falling heavily, so he called the country Snowland. Nonetheless he had much praise for the country when he reached the Faroes.

Another Norwegian Viking called Flóki Vilgerðarson heard of the discovery and determined to settle in this new country. He held a great sacrifice, and dedicated to Óðin three ravens he intended to use as guides on the way. He paused at the Faroes on the way, where he

Toy wooden horse
from Kvívík

married off one of his daughters; one of her descendants was said to be Thránd of Gata, of *Færeyinga Saga*. Flóki then set sail for the north-west. When he was some way out he released one of the sacred ravens, which promptly headed straight back for the Faroes. Later he released the second of the ravens, which returned to the ship. When he released the third raven, it flew off towards some distantly-sensed land far ahead, and now Flóki knew he was on the right way.

When he reached Iceland he sailed along the south coast and into the inviting bays of the west country. He and his companions found the waters teeming with fish. They spent all summer fishing to their hearts' content, but neglected to make any hay for the livestock they had brought with them. It was a hard winter and a late spring, and all their beasts died. While the northern fjords were still choked by sea-ice Flóki made haste to leave. He named the country Iceland, and when he reached Norway he did not have a good word to say for it. One of his companions tried to give a more balanced view, saying that it had advantages as well as disadvantages; but another companion, a man called Thórólf, had been entranced by it, and said that butter dripped from every blade of grass. So Thórólf was nicknamed Thórólf Butter, while Flóki became known as Raven-Flóki.

The story of Raven-Flóki smacks of legend-making, and indeed another tradition indicates that he did settle in Iceland. Whatever the truth of it, Iceland had received its misleadingly chilly name; but in the next few years, a host of Norse immigrants were to follow in his wake, hoping to find more butter than ice.

6

Iceland: a Nation is Born

Iceland is the only country in Europe that remembers its beginnings as a nation, enshrined in the works of her early historians. The first brief history, *Íslendingabók* (Book of Icelanders), was written in Icelandic around 1130 by a priest called Ari the Learned (*fróði*), and not long afterwards he and a group of other scholars compiled the first version of a detailed account of the settlement of Iceland. It is called *Landnámabók* (Book of Settlements), and it records the names and family histories of some four hundred of the chief settlers and their descendants.

It was these early historians who noted that Iceland had first been sighted accidentally by wandering Vikings in the middle of the ninth century, and that Raven-Flóki had attempted to settle there. By that time the sea-routes to the Orkneys and the Faroes were well established, and it was hardly surprising that ships blown off course should come across such a large island.

Iceland's existence was certainly known long before then. It is likely that the Romans knew of it, because four copper Roman coins from the period 270–305 AD have been found amongst ancient Viking ruins in the south and south-east of Iceland, and this time-span covers the period when the Roman navy in Britain was at its height under the command of Carausius; it is not an unreasonable assumption that the coins were brought and left by sailors on board some long-range patrol boat.

Irish hermits, too, had found their way to Iceland by the end of the eighth century, just as they had found their way to the Faroes. In his *Liber de Mensura Orbis Terrae* in 825 Dicuil recorded this early glimpse of Iceland:

Iceland in the Viking Age

'It is now thirty years since priests who lived in that island from the first day of February to the first day of August told me that not only at the summer solstice, but in the days on either side of it, the setting sun hides itself at the evening hour as if behind a little hill so that no darkness occurs during that very brief period of time, but whatever task a man wishes to perform, even to picking the lice out of his shirt, he can manage it as precisely as in broad daylight . . .'

The early Icelandic historians also recorded the presence of Irish hermits in Iceland when the first Norsemen arrived. They had gone there in search of solitude and now left hurriedly, taking with them their only worldly possessions—'bells, books, and croziers, from which one could know that they were Irish'.

News of this empty island spread quickly throughout Norway and the Norse domains in Scotland and Ireland, and a wave of settlers set out for Iceland. Land-shortage must have been one of the causes, but there was also political pressure to contend with in the homeland, where King Harald Fine-Hair was ruthlessly subjugating the whole of Norway under his authority and making punitive raids on the Viking settlements in the Northern Isles and Hebrides. Men who had been used to leading independent lives as chieftains with unchallenged local supremacy resented the new tyranny of the crown. And for those in trouble of any kind, Iceland beckoned as an ideal place of refuge.

According to *Íslendingabók* and *Landnámabók*, the first permanent Norse settler in Iceland was a man called Ingólf Arnarson, who came from the west of Norway. He and his family had fallen foul of a chieftain in the district, and so they decided to emigrate. Ingólf had a foster-brother called Leif, who joined a Viking expedition to the British Isles in order to provide himself with extra means for the voyage. There he acquired ten Irish slaves and plundered a burial mound from which he looted a fine sword; from then on he was known as Hjörleif (Sword-Leif).

A sense of destiny lay over the whole enterprise. Ingólf was a devout pagan, and before he embarked on the journey to Iceland he held a great sacrifice to the gods; but Hjörleif refused to take part in the ceremony, and was later to pay the penalty. Learned men said, 'It is seven days' sail from Stad in Norway to Horn in the east of Iceland,' but in rough weather it could take much longer, and on the voyage across the North Sea Ingólf and Hjörleif lost touch with one another's ships. Hjörleif made land on the south coast of Iceland, at a place still called Hjörleifshöfði (Hjörleif's Head); there his Irish slaves took their revenge and killed him, and fled to the group of islands just off the south coast, the Vestmannaeyjar (Westman Islands), so named in their memory. When Ingólf eventually found his foster-brother's body he pronounced the moral: 'This is what happens to those who will not sacrifice to the gods.'

Ingólf himself had made no such mistake. As he approached the coast of Iceland, he had prudently offered hostages to fortune in a ritual that was to be followed by many later settlers: he threw overboard the carved wooden pillars of his high-seat from his home in Norway. These high-seat pillars were dedicated to the gods, and he vowed that he would make his home wherever the pillars were washed ashore, for the gods would guide them to a place that was acceptable to the guardian spirits of the new country.

It took Ingólf three years to find them again, during which he moved slowly westwards along the south coast. Eventually he came across them lying on the shore of a peninsula in a beautiful wide bay on the west coast of Iceland, ringed by distant blue mountains. On

87

Looking for Ingólf
Arnarson's farm in the
centre of Reyjavík.
On the far left, tell-
tale shadows in the
soil indicate the
remains of very early
turf walls.

all sides he could see steam rising from the ground, the vapour of
innumerable natural hotsprings. So he named the place Reykjavík
(Steamy Bay), and there he built his home. The year, according to
tradition, was 874. More than two centuries later his compatriots
were still so impressed by the manner of his settling that they re-
recorded the fact that 'those high-seat pillars are still there in the
farmhouse'.

Today, by a coincidence of history, Reykjavík is the capital of Iceland. In the heart of the Old Town, surrounded by a clutter of colourful traditional buildings, Icelandic archaeologists have been searching for traces of this original settlement whenever redevelopment allows them access to the ground under the buildings in Aðalstræti (Main Street).

Within a radius of a hundred yards, excavations and test boreholes have produced evidence of very early human occupation: a 'floor layer' of beaten earth, and the bones of many domestic and wild animals and birds including pigs, walrus, and Great Auks. Remains of a stone ember-pit or hearth and other building stones have been found, as well as fragments of some iron utensils and chips of whittled wood. Radiocarbon tests indicate that these deposits are consonant with a date of 870 or even earlier.

In addition to this, the excavators recently found traces of a turf wall at the earliest occupation level. Amongst the grass roots of the turves could be seen traces of volcanic ash (tephra), and it is believed that this ash came from a volcanic eruption in the Torfajökull area, in southern Iceland, shortly before 900. It is on such minute scraps of evidence that archaeologists often have to base their deductions. There is not the slightest chance of finding anything as romantic or substantial as Ingólf's high-seat pillars; but Þór Magnússon, the Director of the National Museum of Iceland, is satisfied that the remains found so far are from a very early Viking Age farm, and sees no reason to doubt that this was the site where Ingólf settled.

A host of immigrants followed Ingólf. The settlement of Iceland seems to have been more or less completed in the sixty years between 870 and 930, by which time it is estimated that the population had grown to 10,000 at least.

They did not come in Viking longships like the Gokstad Ship. The boat that carried the settlers more than 600 miles west from their homeland was a buxom, swan-breasted cargo-boat called a *knörr*. She was a plain and unadorned tramp specifically designed for the deep-sea routes. Her bulky lines were ample and functional, and the greatest compliment that could be paid to a generously-endowed woman was to call her '*knörr*-breasted'.

She was the maid-of-all-work of the northern seas; but no one knew what she was really like until a *knörr* was salvaged, along with four other Viking ships, from the shallow waters of Roskilde Fjord in Denmark in 1962. They had all been scuttled in the middle of the eleventh century to block a navigational channel against raiders, but

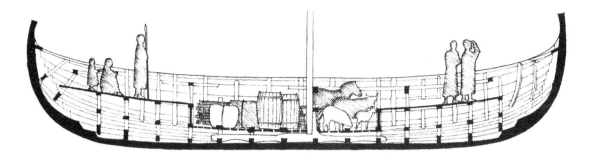

The *knörr*: a reconstruction of the type of ship that pioneered the Atlantic trade routes.

now the *knörr* stands resurrected in the Viking Ship Museum that was specially built in Roskilde to house the ships.

She was built of pine and oak, more than fifty feet long, with a fixed half-deck at prow and stern and an open hold amidships. The hold would be filled with cargo and provisions for the voyage—barrels of water and meal, household equipment and farm implements for the new life that lay ahead. Everything would be stowed under hides, and there would be a huddle of seasick cows and sheep to stock the new farm. On board would be about twenty people, the family and its farmhands. Conditions were cold and uncomfortable; there was no way of cooking food on board, and at night everyone would crowd together in sleeping-bags under a makeshift awning.

The captain would stand on the afterdeck at the steering-paddle that was ingeniously mounted on the starboard ('steerboard') side. A large square sail bulged from the single mast amidships, rigged obliquely to catch a wind on the beam by means of a special spar called the *beiti-áss*. There was no rowing done on the voyage; there were only a few oar-holes in the gunwales fore and aft, and oars were only used in harbour.

To navigate, the settlers used the Pole Star at night and the sun by day. They sailed along latitude 64, due west, keeping position by observing the sun's maximum height at noon and thereby calculating their latitude by comparison with other known places. When the sky was overcast they might have been able to locate the precise position of the sun by scanning the sky through a 'sun-stone' (*sólarsteinn*), a translucent piece of calcite (Iceland spar) whose crystalline structure polarised the light and became opaque when turned towards the invisible sun. Certainly this technique was known in the days of St Olaf, King of Norway (1014–30): one of the sagas tells the story of how Olaf was sailing one day in fog and heavy snow. The mate of the ship was able to locate the sun, 'and then the king picked up the sun-stone and saw how the stone was radiating, and from that he concluded that this was true.'

The early settlers were not at all like the traditional image of bloodthirsty Vikings. The majority of the incomers were from western and southern Norway, but large numbers came from the Norse-occupied regions of the British Isles—the Orkneys and Shetland, the Hebrides, northern Scotland, and Ireland. These first- and second-generation Norsemen brought a generous admixture of Celtic blood and Celtic culture, and often a measure of Christianity to leaven the undemanding paganism of the others.

The archaeological record suggests that paganism was never very deeply rooted in Iceland. Only some two hundred pagan graves have been found, and curiously enough very few are in the western parts of Iceland, which suggests a concentration of Christian settlements in that area. The pagan graves that have survived show that the burial customs were modelled on those of Norway. The dead were provided with their personal ornaments and weapons; elegant bronze brooches in the characteristic Jellinge style have been found in several graves dating from the early tenth century, particularly the brooches found at Snæhvamm in Breiðdale in the east. A burial field near Hafurbjarnarstaðir on Miðnes, in the south-west of Iceland, which contained some eight bodies, also preserved a tenth-century sword whose grip was wound with silver thread, and a scabbard-chape in openwork Jellinge style. A small boat-grave for a man and a boy on the banks of Úlfljótsvatn, in southern Iceland, yielded two early tenth-century swords of Anglo-Saxon make.

But the evidence of pagan burial customs is matched by that of early Christian place-names bestowed by the first settlers. The Irish hermits (*papar*) who fled at the arrival of the Norsemen are commemorated by several names with the element *Pap-*, particularly in the south-east where they seem to have clustered. But in the western fjords there are no fewer than fifteen Settlement Age farms with a 'church' (*kirkju-*) element, and there are many others. One farm was called Kristnes (Christ-ness); according to *Landnámabók* the first settler there, Helgi the Lean (*magri*), had been brought up in Ireland and 'had a very mixed faith—he believed in Christ, but invoked Thór for sea-voyages and in times of stress'.

Thór seems to have been the chief god of farmers and seamen, the big, bluff god of strength; Frey was the god of fertility and Óðin the god of poetry and magic, the All-Father who was worshipped by warriors and the aristocracy. Thór was the most popular god amongst the pagans in Iceland, and his mighty hammer was much worn as a charm. Some handsome amulets depicting Thór and his hammer

One of the tenth-century Anglo-Saxon swords found in a small boat burial on the banks of Úlfljóts-vatn.

Whalebone figurine
from Baldursheim,
possibly Thór

have been found in Iceland, notably a small bronze figurine about
three inches high that came from Eyjafjörd in the north of Iceland,
and a beautiful pendant cross of silver ending in a dragon's head.
Some unidentifiable deity, perhaps Thór, is represented on a tiny
whalebone figurine that was found last century in a grave at Baldursheim near Mývatn, in the north of Iceland; it was the central piece
of a set of twenty-four gaming-pieces made of cow-bone, alongside
one throwing die, and was clearly a favourite possession of the man
who was interred in the grave in the tenth century with all his
weapons and his horse lying at his feet.

The intermingling of culture and religion amongst the early
settlers is exemplified in one large family whose fortunes are recorded
in *Landnámabók* and several later sagas: the family of Ketil Flat-Nose.

Ketil Flat-Nose was a powerful chieftain in Romdalsfjord in west
Norway. He himself may have been of Lappish origin if his nickname
is anything to go by. He was a Viking of the old school, a veteran of
many freebooting forays to Scotland and Ireland. With the rise to
power in Norway of King Harald Fine-Hair late in the ninth century
he decided to emigrate rather than submit to this new royal authority.
He had five children, two sons and three daughters. One son had
been fostered in Sweden, and so was called Björn the Easterner
(*austræni*). The second son had a nickname that sounds Celtic—
Helgi Bjólan. One daughter, Auð the Deep-Minded (*djúpúðga*), was
married to a Norse king in Ireland, Olaf the White (Irish *Amblaibh
conung*), and according to later traditions was a Christian. Another
daughter was married to Helgi the Lean of the mixed faith, who was
the grandson of another Irish king, Kjarval (*Cearbhall*) of Ossory.
The third daughter had a son called Ketil the Foolish (*fíflski*), so
nicknamed because he was a devout Christian.

When Ketil Flat-Nose decided to emigrate, the question was where
to go. The settlement of Iceland was just starting, and Helgi Bjólan
was eager to go there, for he had heard that there was plenty of free
land for the taking and excellent fishing all around. But Ketil, the old
Viking, said contemptuously, 'That fishing-place will never see me
in my old age.' The family split up, Ketil Flat-Nose deciding to go
to Scotland with two of his daughters, while his sons emigrated direct
to Iceland with their brother-in-law Helgi the Lean. The grandson,
Ketil the Foolish, also found his way to Iceland, and earned the
amused contempt of his pagan neighbours by naming his settlement
farm Kirkjubær (Church Farm).

Meanwhile Ketil Flat-Nose settled down in Scotland, all past sins forgiven, and lived there until his death. In Ireland his daughter Auð the Deep-Minded and her husband King Olaf the White trained their son to carve out kingdoms for himself, which he later did to such good purpose in Scotland that the Scots eventually killed him in Caithness.

This left his mother in something of a quandary. She was in Scotland at the time, and had no one else to turn to, for her father was dead by then and her husband had mysteriously vanished from the scene. But Auð the Deep-Minded was nothing if not resourceful. Old as she then was, she had a boat built secretly in a forest, and when it was ready she loaded it with treasure and set sail for the north, taking with her a brood of grand-daughters and a handful of nobly-born slaves her son had captured. She paused in the Orkneys to marry off one grand-daughter into the ruling family of Earls, then paused in the Faroes to marry off another, and finally headed for Iceland. She took her time before deciding where to settle, slowly studying the broad fjords and deep fertile valleys of the west coast before making up her mind. Finally she laid claim to a huge area of land which she then parcelled out to the nobly-born captives who had helped her

A smith in his forge: detail from the carved portal of the Hylestad stave-church in Norway.

escape from Scotland and to whom she now gave their freedom. That done, she settled back to live out the rest of her life in high dignity and comfort, the matriarch of a prolific and cosmopolitan line whose scions would later be immortalised in the great sagas like *Njál's Saga* and *Laxdæla Saga* and *Eyrbyggja Saga*.

These early Icelanders lived in considerable style. *Laxdæla Saga* describes the magnificent timber residence built by one of Auð the Deep-Minded's descendants, Ólaf the Peacock (*pái*), in the second half of the tenth century. It was called Hjarðarholt (Herds' Wood), and stood in a clearing in the woods that once clothed the valley of Laxárdale in the western dales. The great hall was panelled with carved scenes from mythology, including Baldur's funeral, the swimming contest between Heimdall and Loki, and Thór's fishing-trip to catch the World Serpent. More than a thousand guests, says the saga, were entertained at the funeral feast that Ólaf the Peacock held at Hjarðarholt in memory of his father. No trace of that original house remains today, but a series of carvings on the west portal of the Hylestad stave-church in Setesdal, Norway, depicting scenes from the life of the legendary Sigurd the Volsung, may give some idea of what Hjarðarholt looked like in its heyday.

No buildings on such a generous scale as Hjarðarholt have been traced by archaeologists in Iceland, and *Laxdæla Saga* may well have been exaggerating. But at the turn of the century a large hall was excavated at a farm called Hofsstaðir (Temple Stead) near Mývatn in the north. It was forty yards long, built of stone and turf, with a small ante-chamber at one end and a large cooking area a few yards away. It was quite narrow, just over twenty-six feet broad, and it seems to have been the banqueting hall of a chieftain of some standing, but it could not have seated more than a hundred guests at the most. This building was originally interpreted as a pagan temple, perhaps through association with the name of the farm, but scholars now agree that it was only a farmhouse.

Iceland does, however, boast the best preserved Viking Age farmhouse yet found anywhere. It has been called Iceland's Pompeii, for it was due to the activity of the volcano Hekla in the south of Iceland that it has survived. Hekla erupted in 1104, covering a vast area all around with a deep shroud of light-coloured tephra (volcanic ash). One of the twenty farms in the valley of Thjórsárdale buried by that eruption was called Stöng. It was excavated in 1939 by a joint Scandinavian team of archaeologists, and the site is now maintained under cover as a showpiece for the public.

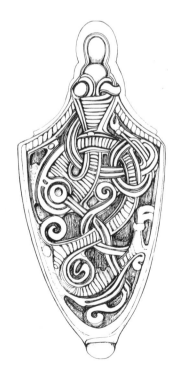

Chape of a sword scabbard from Hafurbjarnarstaðir in Jellinge style

The farmhouse at Stöng had been built in the traditional Icelandic
fashion with thick walls of turves laid on two courses of rough stones.
Although Iceland was well wooded when the first Norsemen arrived,
the trees were mainly dwarf birch and willow and unsuitable for
building, and the volcanic stone on the island was just as unsuitable
for large scale masonry work. The farmhouse consisted of two main
rooms, 'long-houses', placed end to end, and two smaller back-houses
leading off at right angles. The larger hall (*skáli*) is of considerable
size, fifty-five feet long and twenty feet broad. The hearth was a
long fire-place down the centre of the room, and down each side ran
a broad raised earthen side-floor, or dais, which would have been
boarded over and on which the members of the household sat for
their meals during daytime and slept at night. The walls had originally been wainscotted, and there was a clear space between the
panelling and the turf walls to prevent rotting. There was only one
outside door to the hall, with a paved entrance leading into a vestibule,
and this area may have been partitioned off as sleeping-quarters for
the head of the household and his wife.

At the inner end of the hall a doorway leads into the living-room
(*stofa*). This was primarily a work-room and perhaps the kitchen as
well, and was once wainscotted all over, with narrow benches along
the wall. The fire-place was a sunken stone box in the centre.

One of the back-houses was a dairy (*búr*). At the inner end, three
circular impressions in the earthen floor indicated the position of
huge wooden vats that were used to store curdled milk (*skyr*) and

other dairy produce. The other back-house seems to have been a lavatory. It has deep stone-set runnels along both walls. The size of this lavatory, if that is what it was, suggests that the household must have been quite numerous.

A little distance from the dwelling-house were the outbuildings. There was a barn or storage shed, a cow-byre (*fjós*) with a paved central alley with stalls of upright stone slabs on either side to accommodate twenty head of cattle, and also a smithy (*smiðja*). It had a sunken fire-box, a cooling-vat in which to plunge the hot metal, a large anvil-stone, and a small stone quern for grinding coloured volcanic stone to make dyes. There was also a large quantity of bog-iron ore, from which Icelandic farmers made their implements.

The occupants of the farm had clearly had warning of the impending disaster in 1104, for they had time to take away with them all their movable goods and chattels. All they left behind were the discarded bric-à-brac of any household—broken bone combs, a bronze pin, an arrow-head, a broken iron key, a spear-head, and an ice-crampon. But standing in this capacious farmhouse it is not difficult to visualise the daily life of its occupants before the volcano destroyed the valley pastures and buried their home.

Like all Icelandic households it had to be self-sufficient, for there were no villages at all and each farm had to be economically and culturally viable. In these upland valleys the agriculture was mainly pastoral. Some cereals were grown, but the summers were short and the most important crop was hay to feed the cattle and sheep during the winter. Dairy produce was an important part of the economy, but the mainstay of the farm was the rearing of sheep. In the living-room at Stöng, the womenfolk worked the wool all the year round—and very hard work it was, too. They spun the wool on a distaff and spindle, holding the distaff in the crook of one arm and making the spindle start spinning with the other hand. The spindle, weighted by a stone disc (spindle-whorl), sank slowly to the floor, drawing the wool out into a thread, which would then be wound into a ball round a bobbin that was usually the knuckle-bone or vertebra of a sheep. The yarn was woven into cloth on a heavy upright loom that stood in the far corner of the room. Two sets of warp-threads hung from the beam at the top, kept taut by heavy stones hanging from them (loom-weights); the weft was slipped through them and beaten upwards with a weaving-sword made of wood or whalebone. To make one length of this homespun cloth, the women had to walk several miles to and fro across the face of the loom, holding the

OPPOSITE
Above The thirteenth-century Viking cathedral (*foreground*, *left*) at Kirkjubö in the Faroes.
Below The view from Eirík the Red's homestead at Brattahlíð in Greenland. In the foreground are the ruins of a fourteenth-century church.

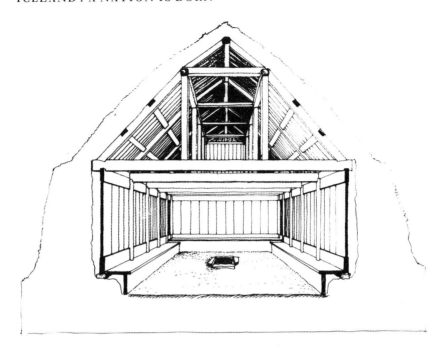

An architect's reconstruction of the small living-room at Stöng.

weaving-sword above their heads to beat the weft into place. It was exhausting work, but it had to be done, for the homespun cloth (*vaðmál*) was one of Iceland's staple exports and a common form of currency as well.

For relaxation in the main hall before the long-fires there were evenings of story-telling, and games like draughts or fox-and-geese played on a gaming-board. The menfolk played a vigorous outdoor ball-game that seems to have been a cross between American football and all-in wrestling. It was played with bats and a hard ball, which could be struck or thrown, with the object of forcing it over the opponents' line. Any number could play at a time, seemingly, and brute strength counted a good deal. Another favourite pastime amongst Icelandic farmers was horse-fighting; two stallions would be matched against each other by their owners and goaded into fighting a duel. It was a matter of great prestige to the owner if his stallion won, and these bouts could often lead to blows long after the horse-fight itself was over.

Thingvellir in Iceland: the lava amphitheatre which saw the birth of the Icelandic republic. The 'Parliament area' was down by the river, below the great rift caused by earthquake subsidence. The flagpole marks the 'Law Rock'.

The sagas are full of incidents of this kind, of sudden brawls that could lead to serious blood-feuds between families; and one of the problems of this pioneer society was law and order. The settlers had come to Iceland in order to get away from enforced authority. They wanted to lead independent lives of their own—but without a king, who was to enforce the law and settle disputes? Who was to punish

97

sheep-stealers and recover runaway slaves?

The earliest settlers had established district assemblies (Things) to deal with local problems and disputes. The earliest recorded district Thing was at Kjalarnes, across the bay from Reykjavík, where the family of the first settler, Ingólf Arnarson, played a leading part. Effective power in each district was in the hands of the main dynastic chieftains, who were called *goðar* (priest-chieftains); they formed an elite oligarchy, and the farmers gave voluntary allegiance and paid temple-dues to the chieftain of their choice in return for protection.

But as the country became more populated, it was inevitable that disputes would arise between men of different districts, for Iceland was never a static community. There were no insurmountable barriers of mountain or river or forest, and ponies and boats made the Icelandic farmer exceptionally mobile. It became obvious that some sort of national authority would be required. In the 920s a man called Grím Goat-Shoe (*geitskór*) reconnoitred the whole of Iceland to acquaint all his countrymen with the proposal to establish a National Assembly and to search for a suitable site. Meanwhile his foster-brother, Úlfljót, prepared a code of laws largely modelled on the Gulathing law-code then current in south-western Norway. But there was one significant difference: no provision was made for a monarchy. Iceland was to be a republic, a commonwealth in which power was to be shared by society, not imposed by royal authority. 'The Icelanders,' wrote the German cleric Adam of Bremen late in the eleventh century, 'have no other king than the laws.'

The site chosen by Grím Goat-Shoe was Thingvellir (Parliament Plains), thirty miles to the east of Reykjavík, a vast natural arena of lava formed by convulsive geological subsidence thousands of years ago when the earth cracked and sank, leaving a huge natural depression twenty-five miles long and six miles broad, bounded on both sides by towering cliffs of riven lava. Here there was plenty of space to house the thousands of people who would flock there, plenty of fresh water, plenty of pasture for grazing horses. It was easy of access and lay close to the most densely populated areas of the country, the south and west, although it took the men from the Eastfjords seventeen days each way to make the journey.

This was the spectacular setting where the new Icelanders held their first National Assembly and became a nation. The traditional date for that momentous occasion is 930. To differentiate it from the local Things, it was known as the Althing (*Alþingi*), and it met in the open air for two weeks every summer.

It has been called the oldest Parliament in Europe, and yet it was not a Parliament in the modern sense of elected representatives. It was the *goðar*, the priest-chieftains, who had the real power. There were thirty-six of them, three for each of the twelve districts into which Iceland was administratively divided, with an elected President or Law-Speaker who held office for three years at a time and whose main function was to recite from memory the whole code of laws, one-third in each year of office. This was a vital task, for the laws were not written down until 1119.

The Althing had both a judicial and legislative function. Court cases were heard in the four Quarter Courts, representing the four major geographical divisions of the country, with ultimate resort to a Court of Appeal called the Fifth Court. But litigation could be a chancy business. Much depended on the power and influence and the size of following of individual *goðar* who could pack the jury and who frequently flouted the court's verdicts. The law-making body was the Legislature (*Lögrétta*), which consisted of all the *goðar* sitting on a wooden platform attended by two non-voting legal advisers. All debates were in public, under the chairmanship of the Law-Speaker, and motions were carried by a simple majority.

The system was imperfect, in that too much power was in the hands of individual chieftains who could, and often did, set themselves above the law. 'Law' in Icelandic meant more than simply rules and regulations; it stood for 'society' as well, the community as a whole, and the worst punishment that could be meted out to an offender was to make him 'out-law', a man outside society whom

Horse-fighting was a popular pastime in Iceland. An illustration from a section governing the rules of the sport in the sixteenth-century vellum copy of *Jónsbók*.

anyone could kill with impunity. But the State had no executive authority to enforce its decisions. There was no bureaucracy, no police force, no army, no king. Court sentences in any given case had to be enforced by the winning side—if it had the strength to do so.

It was this flaw inherent in the system that allowed blood-feuds to flourish in early Icelandic society. A man who felt himself wronged in any way often preferred recourse to the sword rather than the courts, especially if honour was involved. The urgent imperatives of revenge, so deeply rooted in Norse society, overrode all considerations of law and order, and a court verdict involving fines on the offender was never a fully satisfactory substitute for a vengeance killing. The 'honour' of the family demanded blood in exchange for blood.

Yet despite its imperfections, the Althing at Thingvellir was the heart and core of the Icelandic nation for more than three centuries. It was the great annual meeting-place for Icelanders of all walks of life. To Thingvellir every June came the chieftains with their escorts of retainers, sometimes dozens strong. Here came farmers and farmhands, travellers and salesmen, friends and enemies. They lived in substantial stone-and-turf enclosures temporarily roofed with cloth, or else in tents. Thingvellir was both parliament and fairground, senate and circus. Outside the precincts of court and legislature were beer-tents and soup-kitchens, sword-grinders plied their trade, hucksters shouted their wares, young men put on their finest scarlet cloaks and went out to be admired.

Today there are few relics left of all that teeming life that was lived every summer at Thingvellir. A scatter of grass-grown mounds is all that remains of the booths that once housed chieftains and their formidable retinues, and few if any of them can be dated with certainty to the Viking Age. A few years ago a small crozier-head in bronze, shaped like the letter T (tau-cross), was found there when a trench was being dug to take underground cables. It was lying buried some twenty inches below the surface, and has been dated to the second half of the eleventh century. It could well have belonged to a missionary bishop in the early days of the Icelandic Church.

The Church came to Iceland, without bloodshed, at a momentous meeting of the Althing in the year 1000. For some years previously there had been sporadic missionary activity in Iceland, which had met little or no opposition. When King Olaf Tryggvason came to the throne of Norway in 995 this activity was increased, for King Olaf was determined to make his mark on history as the royal evangelist of the North. In Iceland the political implications of this interference from Norway did not go unnoticed, and the country divided into two opposing sides—those who wanted to retain the old ways of easy-going paganism, and the progressives who wanted to bring Iceland into the orbit of Christian Europe. At Thingvellir in 1000 the conflict came to a head; the two parties faced up to each other and a pitched battle seemed inevitable. In the interests of peace, however, a compromise was reached; it was agreed to put the matter to arbitration by the Law-Speaker, even though the Law-Speaker was himself a pagan. He retired to his booth to deliberate for twenty-four hours, and when he emerged he announced his decision: Iceland was to become Christian, but pagans should be allowed to continue practising their old religion as long as they did not offend others thereby. It was a remarkable and probably unique compromise.

It was perhaps not all that surprising in the circumstances. Christianity was already fairly widespread in Iceland; it was simply a matter of systematising it. The pagan priest-chieftains saw where power would lie and took conversion in their stride. The old temples were rebuilt as chapels, and the chieftains' sons took holy orders to ensure their political future. Little changed, except that Iceland ceased to be an outpost, a place of refuge, and became part of the mainstream of European culture.

Fifty years after the Conversion the first native bishopric was established at Skálholt, a historic farmstead in the serene rolling grasslands of the south-west. Skálholt quickly became the religious and cultural powerhouse of the nation, and a succession of notable bishops of great learning and breadth of mind inspired the intellectual life of Iceland during a Golden Age of a hundred and fifty years.

Not long ago, one of these outstanding bishops was resurrected by a happy accident of archaeology. His name was Pál Jónsson, bishop of Skálholt from 1195 to 1211. He was the illegitimate son of a great chieftain and a bishop's sister, educated in England, a layman in minor orders who never intended to make a career in the Church until he was elevated to the episcopal throne by popular acclaim on his uncle's death. He did a great deal to encourage the arts in Iceland and to beautify the timber cathedral at Skálholt, and when he died he was universally mourned.

Before his death, according to his saga, 'he had a fine stone coffin made, in which he was laid when he died'. But as the centuries passed, the site of his last resting-place was forgotten. The bishopric at Skálholt fell into gradual decline until the see was moved to Reykjavík late in the eighteenth century, and all that remained on

The stone coffin of Bishop Pál Jónsson, now in the crypt of the new memorial church at Skálholt.

the site was a dilapidated little parish church.

In the summer of 1954 plans were afoot to build a handsome new memorial church at Skálholt to commemorate the 900th anniversary of the foundation of the first bishopric. A team of archaeologists led by Dr Kristján Eldjárn (then Director of the National Museum, now the President of Iceland) took the opportunity of excavating the site to try to determine the size of the successive medieval cathedrals that had stood there in the past. It soon emerged that the cathedral in Bishop Pál's day had been truly enormous by medieval standards, a timber stave-church over fifty yards long, larger than any stave-church built in Norway; it could seat seven hundred people.

While the excavation of the cathedral foundations was in progress, one of the volunteer helpers at the dig jarred his spade on what seemed to be a block of stone at a depth of about two feet. As he scraped away the earth to try to clear it from the ground, he realised that it was much larger than he thought, and had been deliberately shaped by a mason or sculptor. Dr Eldjárn and his colleagues were hastily summoned to the spot; it was the corner of a stone coffin. A few hours later it stood clear: it was a magnificent sarcophagus carved from a solid block of stone, unadorned but handsomely shaped.

A few days later the lid of the coffin was opened at a formal ceremony at Skálholt. Inside lay the skeleton of a middle-aged man who had been five feet seven inches tall. Across his breast lay a bishop's crozier with a carved crook of walrus ivory. There was no episcopal ring on his hand, however, and the probable explanation is that it had been stolen by a grave-robber, for the crozier had been scraped with a knife as if to see whether it was made of precious metal. The skull rested on a stone pillow, and dust from the lid had settled on it, giving it a golden hue.

Without a doubt the skeleton was that of Bishop Pál, the only bishop to have been buried in a sarcophagus. The style of the ornamentation of the crozier pointed to a date in the late twelfth century, and Bishop Pál's saga records that the ecclesiastical carvings at Skálholt were done by the finest craftsman of the day, a woman called Margrét the Skilful. Today Bishop Pál lies in his sarcophagus in the crypt of the new memorial church at Skálholt, the only person from the Saga Age of Iceland who has been positively identified.

The early Church had inspired a great flowering of the arts in Iceland. Bishop Pál himself had been a notable patron. The few surviving church art-works show how Viking art was transformed in Iceland into a vigorous native idiom.

Four fragments of wood panelling from an old farmhouse at Flatatunga in the north represent all that is left of a large-scale Byzantine vision of the Day of Judgement. The figures of the saved and the damned are plainly carved in the familiar Ringerike style with its trailing tendrils, and the faces of both the Virgin Mary and the Devil can be identified. The panelling had obviously come from a church originally, and dates back to the earliest days of Christianity in the eleventh century.

Much more ambitious and sophisticated is a magnificent carved door that came from the church at Valthjófsstaðir in eastern Iceland; it dates from about 1200, when Pál Jónsson was bishop at Skálholt. It is made of fir and decorated with Romanesque roundels in relief. The lower roundel is an intricate pattern of four dragons interlaced, a throwback to the intertwined 'gripping-beasts' of ninth-century Viking art. The upper roundel depicts the classic medieval theme of the Knight and the Lion: in the lower half the knight on horseback attacks a dragon while a lion gratefully escapes from its clutches, in the upper half the lion jauntily accompanies the knight on his way and is then seen lying grieving on the knight's tomb which bears the

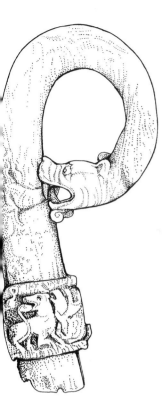

Above Bishop Pál's crozier.
Below Detail of a lioness apparently breathing life into her still-born cubs, to symbolise the Resurrection

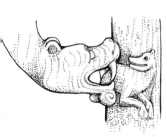

The upper roundel of a carved church door from Val-thjófsstaðir

inscription '[Behold] the mighty king buried here, who slew this dragon'. It is one of the finest examples of medieval woodcarving in northern Europe.

The earliest surviving figure of Christ carved in the round comes from Ufsir in Svarfaðardale in the north of Iceland, and dates from around 1100. It was once part of a crucifix, made of birchwood and carved by a native sculptor in the Romanesque attitude of Christ Triumphant on the Cross. It is a gravely beautiful piece of work.

But the outstanding and most enduring artistic achievement of medieval Iceland was the vernacular literature of the sagas. Two centuries before Chaucer wrote his *Canterbury Tales* the Icelanders

Birchwood figure of
Christ from Ufsir.

were beginning to write prose sagas and histories in their native language; a century before Dante completed his *Divine Comedy* on his deathbed in Ravenna the first major saga masterpiece, *Egil's Saga*, was being written at Reykholt in Iceland.

The art of writing was introduced to Iceland by the Church. Before writing began, the Norsemen used runes, an alphabet of sixteen twig-like letters for carving inscriptions on wood or stone. The use of the runic alphabet, which was thought to have magical associations, survived as a curiosity for several centuries and was common throughout Scandinavia, but it could never serve a purely literary purpose.

Writing quickly became a popular pastime in Iceland, for education was widespread. But it was always a very costly business in those days. Books were written on vellum (calfskin), which required a great deal of skilled preparation as well as a huge quantity of surplus calves—and time. The hide was first shaved with a sharp knife, then scraped and cleaned and then laboriously kneaded by hand to make it smooth and pliable. When the treatment was finished the hide looked like high-quality paper, only softer and much stronger. The writing was done with a quill pen, usually of swans' feathers, using a glossy black ink made by boiling bear-berry plants. Because of the costs involved, the writers tried to get as many words onto a page as possible, and used abbreviations to save space; but there was always room for 'illuminations'—coloured illustrations in the margins and in the texts themselves to embellish the initial letter of a new chapter. One of the most famous of illuminated Icelandic manuscript books, a compilation of sagas and histories known as *Flateyjarbók*, took 113 calfskins to make and more than a year to copy out (it was written in the last decade of the fourteenth century).

Today the Icelandic manuscripts are much discoloured by time and constant handling. In the Middle Ages they were endlessly read, borrowed, and copied, and worn-out books were simply discarded when a new copy was made. With the introduction of paper in the fifteenth century, the old vellum manuscripts lost much of their usefulness, although many of the more important books were kept as family heirlooms in farmhouse libraries all over the country. The new paper manuscripts were much cheaper and much easier to read, for fewer abbreviations were used and the handwriting was less crabbed. When printed books came onto the Icelandic scene late in the sixteenth century, vellum books became even more out of date.

In the seventeenth century, antiquarians began to grow interested in the vellums again because of their antiquity. By then only a tiny fraction of the early manuscripts had survived—just a few fragments from the twelfth century and little more from the thirteenth. The thousands of vellums dating from the fourteenth and fifteenth centuries give only a glimpse of the huge literary industry of Iceland in the Middle Ages, and of the countless calves who gave their lives to it.

But even fewer manuscripts would have survived to this day had it not been for the efforts of the seventeenth-century collectors.

Most of them were acquired by an Icelandic bibliophile called Árni Magnússon, a professor at the University of Copenhagen who spent years travelling round Iceland preparing a land census. In those years he accumulated every scrap of vellum and every paper copy he could lay his hands on, tracking them down in the most unlikely places sometimes: one page of vellum he found had been cut to make an insole for a shoe, another had been trimmed by a tailor to make a pattern for the back of a waistcoat. Árni Magnússon shipped all the manuscripts to his private library in Copenhagen, where part of the collection was destroyed in the great fire of Copenhagen in 1728. He bequeathed what was left to the University of Copenhagen, which was also Iceland's university since Iceland was by then a Danish colony. Now that Iceland is once again an independent nation, the Danish Parliament has made the unparalleled gesture of agreeing to return the majority of the manuscripts to Iceland.

The saga literature of Iceland grew out of the early historical writings of men like Ari the Learned early in the twelfth century. But it was not until the thirteenth century that the major epics were written, the Family Sagas like *Egil's Saga* and *Laxdœla Saga* and *Njál's Saga*, written by Icelanders about the heroes and dynasties of the Viking Age in Iceland and abroad.

In the past the sagas were accepted as literal truth, pure gospel history. But modern scholarship, less biased perhaps, now sees them as dramatised narratives freely based on historical events and personages. The accounts are so vivid and circumstantial that they give every appearance of being factual. One can stand today at the sites where these happenings are said to have occurred and recognise every detail of landscape as described by the saga authors seven centuries ago and more. So it is little wonder that people have looked to archaeology to provide 'proof' that the events really took place.

In *Njál's Saga*, for instance, the climax of the story is the burning to death of Njál and his violent sons in their home at Bergthórshvoll, on the south coast of Iceland, in the year 1011. It was the outcome of a long and bitter blood-feud between the Njálssons and a neighbouring family. Njál had done everything he could to heal the breach, but when a final attempt at reconciliation through a court arbitration at the Althing failed, the fate of his sons was sealed.

The saga sets the scene with great dramatic effect. It is six o'clock on a Monday evening in August. A confederacy of enemies, a hundred strong, has gathered at Berthórshvoll. When frontal attack fails they set fire to the house. The wind is from the east that day, which allows one male member of the family, Njál's son-in-law, to escape under cover of the smoke and later take a terrible revenge; but Njál himself and his wife and sons die as the buildings are burned to ashes.

There is no doubt at all that the Burning was a historical event, for it is mentioned in many other sources. But the thought of finding physical traces of it has prompted a number of people to excavate in the area of the present farmhouse at Bergthórshvoll. The latest comprehensive excavation was undertaken in 1951, when an area to the west of the present buildings was investigated; if the wind had been from the east that evening in 1011, then anything to the west of the dwelling-house would have burned down, too. There was great excitement when charred timbers were found at a depth of some six feet below the surface. Could this have been where Njál had lain down on his bed to die in his blazing house? It turned out that the building had been a cow-byre forty-five feet long, with wooden stalls to accommodate thirty head of cattle. It had been burned to the ground, of that there was no doubt; and radiocarbon tests on the charred beams gave a date that was consonant with the date of the Burning—the byre had been built around 970 or 980.

Of the blaze that destroyed the farmhouse, however, no substantial trace has ever been found—perhaps because the site was cleared immediately and a new farmhouse built on top of it, as has always been customary in Iceland. But the romantics seized gratefully on anything that might have any connection with Njál. Traces of burnt barley were found once—and Njál is portrayed in *Njál's Saga* as a progressive farmer who experimented with methods of increasing his grain yield by manuring his fields. There were remains of curdled milk (*skyr*) such as one would expect to find in any farmhouse—but the saga happens to mention that *skyr* had been used by the womenfolk in a vain attempt to douse the flames during the Burning. And there were remains of burnt chickweed: in the saga an old woman called Sæun, who was credited with having second sight, was one day seen beating furiously at a pile of chickweed near the farm. When asked why she replied, 'This chickweed will be used as kindling when they burn Njál inside the house.' And so it was . . .

Hardly any of the saga writers are known by name, for they never signed their work. But one named author towers over the thirteenth century: Snorri Sturluson of Reykholt. At the time when Genghis Khan was trying to conquer the world by force of arms, Snorri Sturluson was trying to subjugate the world to the discipline of

The open-air bathing pool used by Snorri Sturluson at Reykholt in the thirteenth century.

history. His monumental *History of the Kings of Norway* begins with the words 'The orb of the world which mankind inhabits . . .' It is from the first two words, '*Kringla heimsins*', that his history was given the title *Heimskringla*.

Snorri Sturluson was a politician who was also a poet and man of letters, a man of wealth with a taste for the good things of life, a peasant who behaved like a prince, a man with an enormous zest for living who died a squalid death by assassination. He wrote a treatise on poetics, and *Egil's Saga* as well. He very nearly became King, or at least Earl, of Iceland. He left one other memorial to posterity: an open-air bathing pool.

At Reykholt there is a large circular pool behind the present school buildings. It is constructed of hewn blocks of stone with a diameter of nearly twelve feet and a maximum depth of water of about twenty-seven inches. An underground stone-lined conduit brings a supply of hot water from a natural hotspring a hundred yards away, and in the old days this could be tempered at source by the cold water from a brook which is now dried up. The water-supply was controlled by means of a stone slab slotted into the conduit.

It is impossible to tell whether Snorri built this pool himself; but it was certainly there at the time when Snorri was living at Reykholt. The contemporary *Sturlunga Saga* (Saga of the Sturlungs), which covers the events of the thirteenth century in Iceland, describes Snorri sitting in the pool with his cronies one evening in 1228 discussing politics.

It was politics that proved his undoing in the end. Iceland in the thirteenth century was racked with vicious power-struggles between chieftains who had grown too big for the republic to contain. Private armies ranged the country brawling and plundering, treachery and torture became commonplace. Snorri Sturluson left his library to make his bid for power. He failed, and at the age of sixty-two he was attacked by night in his home and murdered in his cellar by his political opponents in 1241.

The death of Iceland's most distinguished man of letters foreshadowed the fall of the republic. In 1262 the Icelanders, exhausted by internal strife, wearily agreed to submit to the authority of the crown of Norway: anything, even a king, was better than the complete breakdown of civil law and order. The saga-writers continued to write; but now they were mourning the end of the spirit of independence that the Vikings had brought with them to Iceland four hundred years earlier.

7

Greenland: the Edge of the World

Past the archipelago of islands that guard the sea approaches to Greenland, huge mountains flank the entrance to Tunugdliarfik. This was the Eiríksfjörd of the Norsemen. The water is strewn with the flotsam of icebergs from a calving glacier somewhere far ahead. The fjord sweeps in a curving run towards the north, bends and bends again. It broadens out; and there on the eastern side, low gravel banks sweep down to the water's edge aflame with purple river beauty, starred with clumps of willow herb and bluebells. An airstrip and a new hotel stand there now, outcome of a wartime hospital base. Its Greenland name is Narssarssuaq (The Big Plain).

On the other side of the fjord, grassy hillsides tumble down to an incredibly green plain by the seashore, inviting the midday sun. The Greenlanders call it Quagssiarssuq (Little Strange Creek). But when the first Norse settler came, he called it *Brattahlíð*: Steep Slope. It was here, in the year 985 or 986, that he founded a Norse colony that was to survive for five hundred years on the edge of the world until it vanished from history. His name was Eirík the Red (*Eiríkur rauði*).

Once again, the Icelandic sagas and early histories are the major source of information about the Norse settlement of Greenland. As usual, they have to be treated with caution, but nothing in the archaeological record contradicts the picture they paint.

Greenland had been sighted by storm-driven mariners from Iceland at least as early as the beginning of the tenth century. An abortive attempt was made to settle on the inhospitable east coast in 978, but the expedition came to grief after only one bitter winter. Some three or four years later, Eirík the Red decided to reconnoitre the west coast. He had time on his hands, for he had been banished

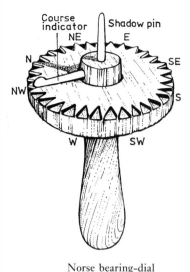

Norse bearing-dial

from Iceland for three years for some killings. He spent his exile to good purpose exploring the western fjords with their unexpectedly fertile valleys tucked in the folds of icy mountains. When he returned to Iceland he spread the news that there was good land for the taking—a vast new country he named Greenland, because 'people would be the more tempted to go there if it had an attractive name'.

He found no lack of volunteers to follow him. The western parts of Iceland were by then becoming overpopulated. All the best land had long since been taken in the first rush of settlement, and successive years of famine in the 980s made for hard times. So when Eirík the Red went back to Greenland he was accompanied by a flotilla of twenty-five ships both large and small, carrying three hundred would-be colonists from the western districts of Iceland. They were the first European settlers to migrate with all their possessions and livestock to found a permanent colony across the Atlantic. But of that brave fleet, only fourteen ships reached their destination: the others either foundered in some freak disturbance of the sea or were forced back to Iceland. A Hebridean poet on board one of them tried to allay his fears of the Greenland voyage with a lay addressed to the Creator, the oldest surviving Christian verse-prayer in Icelandic:

> 'I beseech the immaculate Master of Monks
> To steer my journeys;
> May the Lord of the lofty heavens
> Hold His strong hand over me . . .'

It was a hazardous journey at the best of times, through the fogs and ice-floes of the Denmark Straits round Cape Farewell: four days in good weather, an eternity in bad. Even in perfect visibility they were out of sight of land for twenty-four hours. But aboard the swan-bosomed *knörr* they now had an instrument of incalculable value—a bearing-dial by which to establish the points of the compass by reference to the sun. An Icelandic astronomer of the late tenth century, Stjörnu-Oddi (Star-Oddi), had compiled a set of tables giving the height of the midday sun for every week throughout the year, expressed in terms of 'half-wheels' (half the apparent diameter of the sun). A half of a notched wooden disc found in a Norse ruin in Greenland in 1948 suggests how these tables were put to practical use. The disc had sixteen equidistant notches round the outside; when whole it would have corresponded to the 32-point division of the horizon current in late medieval times. It had a hole in the centre which could have taken a handle-shaft with a shadow-pin and a

OPPOSITE
Sixteenth-century illuminated vellum copy of the ancient Icelandic code of laws, *Jónsbók*. This section deals with marriage.

er þingi skal rett taka at konu hinre er
hon er legin. karl mað en eigi kona. þo
at hon sie er þingi. s̄ sa sem iomeygþ e sin
vnllrida z taki uboðs mað þus hint
haða. nea hon eigi ær boða. þa tekur þ
rett at konu hinre. Kona sialf at rett at
ser ef hon e borð z sa hon er eigi bonda
z hin etna þ sin kona uðr barf hafaði
þa sk sa e þ tm at yfia þm z kost e kou
anaðzt með hon u i þui siukleika z e
þ buiþost. Nu ef sa mað e andað e ko
nu hef legin. þa sk er þingi sua þm re
tti z kostnaði e mslu sin hon hef þe tek
ept þ. en e mersa. En augu at þu at
sina þar sin þu er þis eðu

hin þm að
hon þmrað i slut langbok ug sea
ger þmrst u kueia giptui z hu
gip in ss sk ua

ꝼaðir eðs
maðer sk ua rað
giptui dæt sin
na. er þau en t
En er þra miller. þa sk uoð þmð z
maðe hu uenurtu giptigu raða. Hu
e brað uant z skur þa at þa sk sa fa
sin hu raðu fylg er þ þui raþ rx z e
sk hin etna þ sin plei e fa skon t. Hip
tiug mað sk skaha heun fylgiu z til

giop þ snðkau sina. e sin sin kein at
sat þu sku z þa eindaga uær hrullaup
skue. e sk hin at laðu geþt mei til giop
uiep eðu kou. eu til ke hur aða þo að
in sie rik. z þuigi meiua e þuður ur þe
sins. En ef ui geþ i beztu eigu sin þa
sku er þingi þus leysa til sin er þu uit
ra. En ef þa sku at u maldaga. þa la
ti þest mað þe tuegia ui eine uhei
in þylgiu hu uilt u þra e þra u. En ef
þa skur at u til giop. þa mot giptui ui
tuegia uotta u þyira skarði. Eigi skal
i klæðu meira heuua geþazt en þanig
ij eu þ sin mei geþ giptui mað þa sk
ia i þylgm þuigu. at þu megi uða þm
til þra. eðr afla e konu þar. En aug
heuu þylgiu ma ar þu giptigar uiz ui
uþa þa er e giop sin uu uar skilt e
ef kou eðr mær uua ekkia giptizt þ uit
rað þoð z mað. eðr braðu sins. e þll er
giptui ui e þ raði huar. hapi þ gurt
ar þu ept giptui uu þu sin hu stoðt
z neuua ule mei uulku at gio uua gi
ptigar ui uil þuira lsa ra þrædi. þa
ma hu giptazt uu eiua skysam þuða
sina ui. ef sin hst ra þrædi e bet z ui
egu þu u eiði sinu sana. z at þo et lei
ta silla að uið giptui ui. En giptui ui er

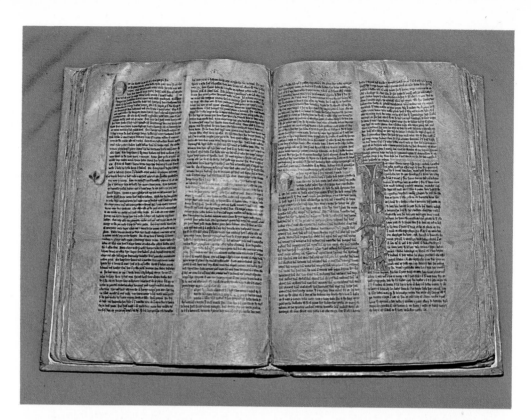

movable course-pointer. The bearing-dial had only to be turned until the notch representing the south was pointing to the spot where a vertical line drawn from the midday sun (as calculated by Stjörnu-Oddi) would intersect the horizon, whereupon the navigator could move the course-pointer, and the prow of his ship, in the desired direction. The sagas say that ships know the way, once they have been; but the bearing-dial was the real reason why the Icelanders were the first people in northern Europe who could sail into the unknown, and find their way back.

When the first settlers arrived in Greenland they split into two groups. The larger group, under Eirík the Red, colonised the Julianehaab district farther to the south (the so-called Eastern Settlement), while the remainder pressed on for another 400 miles up the west coast to found the Western Settlement in the Godthaab district.

They found a land well suited to the kind of farming they had been accustomed to in Iceland. The climate was appreciably warmer than today. The author of the thirteenth-century *Konungs Skuggsjá* (King's Mirror), a book of court etiquette, had heard good reports of it:

'It is reported that the pasturage is good, and that there are large and fine farms in Greenland. The earth yields good and fragrant grass. The farmers raise cattle and sheep in large numbers, and make butter and cheese in great quantities. The people exist chiefly on these foods, but they also eat the flesh of various kinds of game such as caribou, reindeer, whales, seals, and bears.'

Above Flateyjarbók: a magnificent vellum manuscript book written in Iceland late in the fourteenth century. It contains a large number of sagas, including *Grænlendinga Saga*. *Below* Nineteenth-century oil painting by H. Schiett of a typical saga-reading scene in an Icelandic farmhouse.

Apart from the farmlands there were also the Northern Hunting Grounds (*Norðrseta*), which provided valuable materials for export. Trappers went north to fetch walrus ivory and furs and hides. Walrus hides were ideal for manufacturing rigging for ships, for the ropes stayed pliable and strong even in the coldest weather. Captive Greenland falcons and polar bears were much prized as luxury possessions in courts abroad. These pioneer hunters penetrated very far north: a runic inscription from the early fourteenth century found in a cairn on the island of Kingigtorssuaq at latitude 72 degrees 55' reads: 'Erling Sighvatsson and Bjarni Thórðarson and Indriði Jónsson on the Saturday before minor Rogation Day [April 25] piled these cairns and . . .' They were a long way from home.

Brattahlíð, the home of Eirík the Red, was the economic and political centre of the Eastern Settlement. The homestead lay a little way up the slope, facing towards the fjord. Farther along the

The runic inscription
found on a cairn at
Kingigtorssuaq.

shore is the grassy plain on which the Norsemen held their Assembly,
modelled on the local Things of Iceland. Brattahlíð provided the
hereditary chieftain of the Thing.

The house itself is now a low, grass-grown ruin. The oldest part
is a large hall built like a Viking long-house with walls five feet
thick, made of stone and strips of turf. The interior measures nearly
forty-five feet by fifteen. There was a conduit leading water through
the house, and a central hearth—all reminiscent of the oldest house-
ruins found in Iceland.

In front of the house a spring bubbles up, and round it are the
remains of an ancient well-house. Farther down the slope were the
outbuildings of the farm, four barns and two cow-byres, solidly
constructed of turf and stone. The cow-byres could house twenty-
eight head of cattle in stalls partitioned by thin slabs of stone or the
shoulder-blades of whales.

Life at Brattahlíð was busy and prosperous. Spindle-whorls and
loom-weights, steatite cooking-pots and bowls, and stone lamps
fuelled by whale-oil were all found on the site. The kitchen midden
was full of fish and animal bones, particularly the bones of seals, but
the people of Brattahlíð enjoyed a varied diet of caribou, polar bears,
and domestic animals. The stream near the farm teemed with fish,
and pollen analysis of the soil has proved that the settlers grew their
own corn.

Inside the house were found discarded knives and a whetstone,
and some gaming-pieces carved from walrus-bone. In this remotest
corner of European civilisation, life was good. *Eirík's Saga*, one of
the two main documentary sources about the Greenland enterprise,
tells of a winter of feasting at Brattahlíð, with 'much games-playing
and story-telling, and many other entertainments that enrich a
household.'

114

Eirík the Red had a wife called Thjóðhild. According to *Eirík's Saga*, their son, Leif the Lucky, was converted to Christianity in Norway by King Olaf Tryggvason, and returned to Greenland around the year 1000 with a missionary priest to preach the new faith:

'Eirík was reluctant to abandon his old religion, but his wife, Thjóðhild, was converted at once, and she had a church built not too close to the farmstead. This building was called Thjóðhild's Church, and there she and many others who had accepted Christianity would offer up their prayers. Thjóðhild refused to live with Eirík after she was converted, and this annoyed him greatly.'

But where was Thjóðhild's Church? The ruins of a large stone church lie just below the farmstead of Brattahlíð, rectangular in shape and constructed of big blocks of red sandstone. The architectural style proves that it cannot have been built earlier than about 1300, and besides it was much too close to Eirík's homestead to fit the saga account.

The answer came in 1961, when some workmen were digging trenches for the foundations of a school hostel about two hundred

The remains of the hall at Brattahlíð, where the colonisation of Vínland was planned.

Some of the skeletons from the graveyard round the tiny church built by Thjóðhild at Brattahlíð.

yards to the south of the farm. Suddenly they started unearthing human skulls; they had struck an ancient cemetery. When the skulls were shown to be of Nordic, not Eskimo, origin, archaeologists from the Danish National Museum were called in.

In the middle of this graveyard they found the remains of a tiny chapel built chiefly of strips of turf fortified with stones. The walls formed the shape of a U, but the west gable was made of wood, like some of the little country churches in Iceland. The interior, paved with red sandstone flags, measured only eleven feet by six, giving room enough for only a score of people standing shoulder to shoulder to listen to the priest officiating in the tiny chancel at the far end.

It stood just inside the turf dyke of the homefield of Brattahlíð, 'not too close to the farmstead'. It was undoubtedly Thjóðhild's Church—the earliest surviving Viking Age church ever found.

All around lay buried the skeletons of some 150 people, the first Viking settlers of Greenland, women to the north, men to the south. Leif the Lucky, the first explorer of North America, must lie buried here, and also Thjóðhild herself, perhaps in the important grave-plot just beside the door.

But not, presumably, Eirík the Red. The saga says he was still a pagan when he died—and in the ruins of Brattahlíð, they found a broken piece of steatite with the emblem of Thór's Hammer incised on it.

Greenland was the staging post for the last fling of the Viking impetus towards the West. It was in the great hall of Brattahlíð that the exploration and settlement of Vínland (North America) was

Thjóðhild's Church would have looked very like this small country chapel at Núpsstaður in the south of Iceland.

planned, and it was from the ship-haven at Brattahlíð that the first trans-Atlantic sea-route was pioneered.

Another farm in Greenland also had a part to play in the Vínland venture: the farm of Herjólfsnes (modern Ikigait, the Burnt Homestead), right at the southern point of the Eastern Settlement. For this was where the accidental discoverer of Vínland came home to safety.

His name was Bjarni Herjólfsson. According to *Grænlendinga Saga* his father Herjólf was one of the emigrants who had gone to Greenland with Eirík the Red. This Herjólf had made his home at Herjólfsnes. His son Bjarni was a merchant who plied the trade-routes from Iceland to Norway, and he was abroad when his father sold up and emigrated. Finding his father gone, Bjarni decided to follow him to Greenland, but his ship was blown wildly off course across the Atlantic. There he caught sight of lands that no European had set eyes on before; but mindful of his cargo, and cautious by nature, he did not pause to investigate, but hurried back towards Greenland and made land at Herjólfsnes. He had had greatness thrust upon him, and spurned it: 'Bjarni now gave up trading and stayed with his father, and carried on farming there after his father's death.'

However, apart from the Vínland enterprise, Greenland was a Viking community in its own right. By a freak of climate, archaeologists have been presented with an unexpected bonus at Herjólfsnes, because in the late Middle Ages the weather all over Europe began to deteriorate. In Elizabethan times the winters in England grew so cold that the Thames sometimes froze over and oxen were roasted on the ice in public barbecues. This change of climate is called the Little European Ice Age. Its effect on Greenland was to turn a country that had been marginally inhabitable into one that was uninhabitable for Europeans. But the perma-frost that set in helped to preserve the cemetery at Herjólfsnes and thereby add greatly to our knowledge of medieval Europe in the form of a unique wardrobe of clothes—the clothes that the dead had been buried in. There were thirty dresses, seventeen hoods, six stockings, and five hats. They were made from the staple Greenland home-made twill, and tailored with great skill. The women's dresses were narrow-waisted with full skirts, with low rounded necklines and full- or threequarter-length sleeves. They date from the fourteenth century, when men in Greenland apparently wore similar robes—a far cry from the tunic and trousers of the earlier Viking period.

The hoods were embellished with long streamers of a kind often seen in medieval portraits but never seen in practice until now. They are called 'liripipe' hoods, and they were the height of fashion in the fourteenth century—so much so that bishops had occasion to rebuke their clergy for wearing their liripipes too long. Greenland was not so remote from Europe in those days as one might imagine.

At the height of its prosperity the Viking colony in Greenland probably numbered at least three thousand people. The written sources mention by name 190 farms in the Eastern Settlement around Brattahlíð, and ninety more in the Western Settlement farther north. But there must have been many more, and already the traces of some three hundred farms have been indentified, and many have been excavated. They were built in every nook and cranny, wherever there was grass to graze the livestock.

Medieval clothing preserved by the perma-frost in the cemetery at Herjólfsnes.

119

Polar bear from
Sandnes carved from
walrus ivory.

Excavation has produced a host of domestic implements that give a clear picture of a self-reliant community improvising its implements and its art from materials to hand, like whalebone axes, for instance, to make up for the shortage of iron.

Sculpture in wood and bone was common: not the intricate, intertwined styles of Scandinavia, but a strong clear line not unlike the native Eskimo carvings.

From Umiviarssuk in the Western Settlement came a bearded man's head whittled from a piece of willow branch, and a carefully modelled wooden toy boat, nine inches long, complete with oar-holes and a notch near the stern for the steering paddle. From Sandnes in the Western Settlement came a little carving of a polar bear in walrus ivory, all grace and bulk and power, and a chiselled man's head in ivory. An animal head at the end of the arm of a chair has echoes of the old Ringerike style. But the most memorable of the carvings is the Sandnes Christ, a fine crucifix carved in driftwood, eight inches high, dating from about 1300.

Like Iceland, Greenland had its Golden Age in the eleventh and twelfth centuries, and as in Iceland, it flowered around the Church. Up and down the settlements, nearly a score of churches were built, and a monastery and a nunnery. Early in the twelfth century the Greenlanders decided to ask for a bishopric of their own, and the chieftain of Brattahlíð sailed to Norway to petition the king, taking a live polar bear as a gift. A Norwegian bishop duly arrived in 1126, and established his seat at Garðar (now called Igaliko, 'The Deserted Cooking-Place').

Garðar lies in the middle of the Eastern Settlement within easy reach of Brattahlíð, on the narrow neck of land between Eiríksfjörd and Einarsfjörd. It is a tranquil, sheltered place, surrounded by fertile farmlands; and here the bishopric prospered and grew strong, a classic example of the power and the energy of the medieval Church. Greenland was a republic on the Icelandic model, and in the absence of a royal court, the bishop soon took over as temporal as well as spiritual head of the nation. The assembly site for the district Thing was moved to Garðar, and the traditional Viking chieftains of Brattahlíð were heard of no more.

A magnificent stone cathedral was built at Garðar in the twelfth century, whose ruins still lie tumbled in the midst of a new settlement of Greenlanders who have quarried it zealously for building-stone. It was thirty yards long and eighteen yards broad, constructed of the handsome red-and-white speckled Igaliko sandstone that

The Sandnes Christ.

some call Igaliko marble. The largest blocks weigh up to ten tons. The cathedral was dedicated to St Nicholas, patron saint of seafarers. It was cruciform, with a chancel and two side-chapels to the east. Fragments of green glass have been found, proving that the windows had been glazed instead of covered with the opaque animal membrane in use elsewhere in Greenland; and from surviving pieces of bronze it is estimated that the church bell weighed half a ton.

A flagged path led across a courtyard to the episcopal residence, which was part of an impressive complex of buildings forming a hollow square. The bishop's house itself was nearly twice as long as the cathedral. It contained a dozen rooms, of which the largest was a great banqueting hall which could seat several hundred people.

Nearby was a large stone barn whose massive walls are still standing to a height of five feet. This was the bishop's tithe barn, the treasury of the church, in which he stored the tithes from the community—walrus ivory and furs, *vaðmál* cloth and farm produce.

There were two huge cow-byres, one of them the longest Norse structure in Greenland at seventy yards. The bishop had room for a hundred head of cattle, and the grandiose scale of the building gives a striking impression of the prestige and wealth of the bishopric in Greenland, the smallest diocese in Europe. It was a stupendous undertaking for such a small community.

A great number of minor objects were found during the excavation of the whole site in 1926—spindle-whorls, knives, gaming-pieces, and two Viking Age rings, one of twisted gold wire and the other of bronze. And strangely enough twenty-five walrus heads, all minus their precious tusks, and five narwhal skulls were found buried within the chancel of the cathedral as carefully as men of rank.

There was one human burial of note that seemed to link Greenland intimately with Iceland. In a grave in the north-east chapel lay a skeleton that wore a gold episcopal ring. Across the body lay a crozier handsomely carved from walrus ivory.

This man has been associated with Bishop Jón Smyril (Sparrow-hawk), who died in 1209, a contemporary and friend of Bishop Pál Jónsson of Iceland. *Bishop Pál's Saga* records a visit that Bishop Jón Smyril paid to Skálholt one Easter, during which he taught the people there how to make wine from bilberries—a precious skill in a country that had to import all its communion wine; and Bishop Pál loaded him with gifts when he left. It has been suggested that one of the gifts may have been the fine crozier he took to his grave, and that it had been fashioned by Margrét the Skilful, the sculptress who made Bishop Pál's own crozier. The saga records that she had made a particularly beautiful crozier for the Archbishop of Norway, so it is a tempting supposition; but there is no real resemblance between the handiwork and style of the Icelandic and Greenland croziers, and the identification of the grave with that of Bishop Jón Smyril is probably a romantic illusion.

Greenland came under the rule of the Norwegian crown in 1261. In return for the taxes he would collect, the King of Norway promised to maintain regular sea communications with Greenland, for the Greenlanders now had no large cargo-boats of their own.

But less than a century later, the more exposed Western Settlement had been abandoned by the Norsemen, perhaps in the face of hostile attacks by the native Eskimos following the game south as the climate worsened. The Norsemen had come across traces of the Eskimos when they first arrived—abandoned boats, for instance—and had also shrewdly deduced they were of the same stock as the natives of North America. They called these absent aborigines *Skrælings*, or 'wretches'.

Viking Greenland was now in inexorable decline, becoming more and more isolated as Europe's merchants lost interest in her markets. Her last written record concerns a fine stone church that stands roofless on the shore of Hvalsey island in the Eastern Settlement. It is the best preserved medieval ruin in Greenland, its walls still standing almost to their full original height.

It was built in the eleventh century, its stones carefully mortared with lime made from burnt mussel-shells. There are two niches in the walls that once held the church plate. The east gable has a handsomely arched window, and four other windows pierce the wall facing the sea. Nearby are the remains of a large complex of a dozen buildings, including a chieftain's hall with standing walls.

There was once a flourishing community on Hvalsey, which certainly survived into the first decades of the fifteenth century. In the year 1406, a ship bound from Norway to Iceland was blown off course to Greenland. It stayed for four years.

It caused a few social upheavals during that time. First, a certain Kolgrím was burned at the stake for witchcraft after seducing the wife of one of the Icelanders on board—she herself is reported to have gone mad soon afterwards and died. And then, in September 1408 a well-born Icelander called Thorstein Ólafsson married a local girl called Sigríð Björnsdóttir. Banns were called, and the whole community came to Hvalsey Church to attend the wedding.

Crozier head of walrus ivory, thought to have belonged to Bishop Jón Smyril

The ruins of Hvalsey
Church today.

When the ship eventually left Greenland, the young couple went with it, and settled in Iceland.

But after that—from Greenland, silence. No more ships approached its shores, no survivors came back to tell the tale. The Eastern Settlement, beleaguered by cold and ice and hostile Skrælings, was never heard of again, and no one knows the fate of this Viking outpost on the edge of the habitable world. Some think the settlers escaped to North America, to start a strain of intriguing folk-memories amongst the Indians. Others think that they went native, abandoning their faith and their Norse traditions, or else that they starved to death, or were exterminated.

There are Eskimo stories about the last Norsemen in Greenland. They speak of an attack by the Skrælings on the last surviving community, on Hvalsey. The Norsemen, it is said, took refuge in Hvalsey Church, but that night the Skrælings set fire to the church. Everyone inside was burned to death except the leader of the Norsemen, a heroic warrior called either Ungortok or Ólaf, who managed to escape through a window with his young son in his arms. The Skrælings pursued him; and after a desperate chase during which he had to abandon his son, they caught up with him at Garðar. And there, in the shadow of the great red sandstone cathedral, they did him to death by sorcery.

In Hvalsey Church there is evidence to show that once upon a time it was burnt.

8

Vínland: North America Discovered

On the northernmost tip of Newfoundland, by Épaves Bay (Wreck Bay), there stands a tiny isolated fishing village called L'Anse aux Meadows. The locals call it Lancy Meadows, thinking that the name is English and reflects the large areas of meadowlands all around, but in fact it is a corruption of the original French name, *L'Anse au Méduse*, meaning Jellyfish Creek.

It was here, in 1960, that a Norwegian explorer and writer called Helge Ingstad was shown a number of grass-grown humps and depressions—slightly raised rectangular outlines which suggested the remains of the walls of some very old buildings. The local fishermen thought they were the remains of houses built by early colonial settlers in the sixteenth century, but Ingstad thought otherwise. For several years he had been intent on trying to find Vínland, the area of North America that Norsemen from Greenland and Iceland had discovered and attempted to colonise round about the year 1000; he had spent the whole of the summer of 1960 exploring the Atlantic coast of North America, trying to follow the rather confused sailing directions recalled in the Icelandic sagas. By the time he reached Newfoundland he had covered many thousands of miles by boat and aeroplane, and was almost ready to give up the search.

The ruins at L'Anse aux Meadows rekindled his enthusiasm. Here, he was sure, was the elusive Norse settlement site that scholars and enthusiasts had been hoping to find for more than a century. In the past, a number of people have claimed to have found Norse remains in North America, but none has stood up to closer investigation. The only way of proving the L'Anse aux Meadows site was by scientific archaeological excavation.

Ingstad is not himself a professional archaeologist—he is a specialist on life in the Arctic; but his wife, Anne Stine Ingstad, had had archaeological training, and so she was appointed to take charge of the digging.

The excavation began in 1961. In all, there were seven seasons of digging between 1961 and 1968, as a result of which Helge Ingstad claimed that he had found the first indisputable Norse remains in North America—the site of the Norse settlement in Vínland.

The story of the Norse discovery and attempted colonisation of North America is told in the two Icelandic sagas that record the settlement of Greenland: *Grænlendinga Saga* (The Saga of the Greenlanders), which was written in Iceland around the middle of the twelfth century, and *Eirík's Saga*, which was written about a century later. *Eirík's Saga* was written as a deliberate revision or 'improvement' of *Grænlendinga Saga* by a learned author who thought he had more reliable sources about the families involved, and this gave rise to several apparent contradictions in the two accounts.

According to *Grænlendinga Saga*, the first accidental discoverer of North America was Bjarni Herjólfsson—the young Icelandic merchant on his way to join his father who had emigrated to Green-

Épaves Bay in Newfoundland.

land with Eirík the Red and settled at Herjólfsnes. This was in the summer of 985 or 986:

> '... They put to sea as soon as they were ready and sailed for three days until land was lost to sight below the horizon. Then the fair wind failed and northerly winds and fog set in, and for many days they had no idea what their course was. After that they saw the sun again and were able to get their bearings; they hoisted sail and after a day's sailing they sighted land. They discussed amongst themselves what country this might be. Bjarni said he thought it could not be Greenland. The crew asked him if he wanted to land there or not; Bjarni replied, "I think we should sail in close." They did so, and soon they could see that the country was not mountainous, but was well wooded and with low hills. So they put to sea again ...'

Thus in sober, almost casual tones, the saga records the first European glimpse of the shores of the New World, five hundred years before Christopher Columbus. But Bjarni was not interested. He knew he was much too far west for Greenland, so he sailed off towards the north-east. Two days later he sighted another country, where once again he refused to land; it was flat and wooded, and he knew it could not be Greenland. Another three days' sail brought him to another country, barren and mountainous, which again he bypassed. Four days later, sailing before a gale, he reached his proper destination—Herjólfsnes in Greenland.

Bjarni's refusal to explore these unknown lands earned him no credit amongst his fellow-countrymen. Greenland was agog with talk of discovering new countries, and it was Eirík's son, Leif Eiríksson, who now took the initiative:

> 'Leif was tall and strong and very impressive in appearance. He was a shrewd man and always moderate in his behaviour.'

He bought Bjarni's ship—perhaps on the principle that 'ships know the way back'—and set off with a crew of thirty-five. This would have been around the year 990.

Without any apparent difficulty they sighted the three countries that Bjarni had seen, but in reverse order. They landed on the first one, found it rocky and barren, and called it *Helluland* (Slab-Land); in all probability this was Baffin Island. The second country, flat and wooded, they named *Markland* (Forest-Land); this is usually identified with the coast of Labrador. After a further two days' sail

Leif the Lucky decides to explore Vínland; Chapter 2 of *Grænlendinga Saga* in *Flateyjarbók*.

before a north-east wind they sighted land again, with an island lying to the north of it:

'They went ashore and looked about them. The weather was fine. There was dew on the grass, and the first thing they did was to get some of it on their hands and put it to their lips, and to them it seemed the sweetest thing they had ever tasted.'

Thus the saga records the reactions of the first Europeans to set foot on the shores of the New World—ocean-weary sailors for whom the taste of fresh dew on the grass remained an exquisite memory. They had come to a land of plenty:

'There was no lack of salmon in the river or the lake, bigger salmon than they had ever seen. The country seemed to them so kind that no winter fodder would be needed for livestock: there was never any frost all winter and the grass hardly withered at all.'

They decided to spend the winter there, and built some large houses. Then Leif organised his men into exploring parties to reconnoitre the hinterland, and it was on one of these expeditions that a member of the crew, a German called Tyrkir, made an exciting discovery: he found vines and grapes growing wild. When Leif and his men sailed away next spring with a full cargo of timber and dried grapes, he named the country with the same flair that his father had shown over Greenland: he called it *Vínland*—Wineland.

Behind him in Vínland he left 'Leif's Houses', as they were called, as his stake in the new country's future, for Vínland could supply many of the resources like wine and timber that Greenland had to import at considerable expense. On his way back home to Greenland he had the good fortune to rescue the crew of a wrecked ship who had taken refuge on a skerry, and for this good deed he earned the nickname *heppni*—'the Lucky'. One of the people he rescued was a woman called Guðríð, who is introduced in the saga without ceremony as the wife of one of the Norwegian survivors of the shipwreck; she became the heroine of the later Vínland adventures, and was destined to be the first recorded white woman to bear a child in the New World.

Thus *Grænlendinga Saga. Eirík's Saga* gives a version that is tantalisingly similar but different in one major respect—the identity of the man who first set eyes on Vínland: not Bjarni Herjólfsson, who is not mentioned at all, but Leif the Lucky.

According to *Eirík's Saga*, Leif went to Norway in the year 999 and stayed as an honoured guest at the court of King Olaf Tryggvason, the royal evangelist whom history has credited with converting all the North Atlantic countries to Christianity. In that same summer, according to *Eirík's Saga*, King Olaf sent Leif back to Greenland to convert the Greenlanders to Christianity in his name:

> 'Leif set sail when he was ready; he ran into prolonged difficulties at sea, and finally came upon lands whose existence he had never suspected. There were fields of wild wheat growing there, and vines, and among the trees there were maples. They took some samples of all these things.'

On the way back to Greenland, just as in *Grænlendinga Saga*, Leif rescued some shipwrecked seamen and thereby earned his nickname of 'the Lucky'. But Guðríð was not amongst them; Guðríð had already been introduced in full saga style as the daughter of a rich Icelandic farmer who had been forced to emigrate to Greenland when he fell upon hard times, and two whole chapters had been devoted to her story. The difference in the two sagas over the treatment of the future heroine of the Vínland voyages is very striking.

In Greenland, Leif went about his mission of converting his fellow-countrymen to Christianity at the Norwegian king's behest, and one of his first converts was his mother, Thjóðhild. It was someone else who now undertook the planned voyage of exploration to follow up the first accidental sighting: Leif's brother, Thorstein Eiríksson. But his expedition never reached Vínland. His ship was storm-tossed all summer:

> 'At one time they were within sight of Iceland; at another they observed birds off Ireland. Their ship was driven back and forth across the ocean. In the autumn they turned back towards Greenland and reached Eiríksfjörd at the beginning of winter, worn out by exposure and toil.'

The crucial difficulty of reconciling the two saga accounts has always been the role played by Leif the Lucky. In *Grænlendinga Saga* he is the man who follows up the chance discovery of another, Bjarni Herjólfsson; in *Eirík's Saga*, he is the chance discoverer, and the follow-up voyages are left to others. In the past, scholars have always preferred the *Eirík's Saga* version, because *Eirík's Saga* is the 'better' saga of the two, by literary standards. *Grænlendinga Saga* was composed in the very earliest period of saga-writing, and is coarse-grained and unsophisticated, whereas *Eirík's Saga* shows all the hallmarks of the classic saga-writing period in the thirteenth century—polished, suave, consciously aware of literary techniques.

This explains why the credit for discovering North America has always been given to Leif Eiríksson rather than to Bjarni Herjólfsson; and when the Americans decided to honour the Norse discovery by designating a special day of celebration, they called it 'Leif Erickson Day'— October 9th, three days before 'Columbus Day' on October 12th.

Bjarni Herjólfsson has now been reinstated as the true discoverer of North America, however, as a result of the work of the late Icelandic historian Professor Jón Jóhannesson. In 1956 he published in Iceland a pioneering essay which clarified beyond reasonable doubt the relationship between the two sagas and explained how the contradiction had come about.

During the thirteenth century, serious attempts were made in Iceland to have King Olaf Tryggvason canonised as the patron saint of the North. Biographies were written in which his pious exploits were eulogised and much exaggerated. He had formerly been credited with the conversion of five countries (Norway, Iceland, the Orkneys, Shetland, and the Faroes), but now a sixth country was added to the list for good measure—Greenland. Professor Jóhannesson traced this story to an Icelandic monk who wrote a Latin biography, now lost, of King Olaf about the year 1200.

By the middle of the thirteenth century, the fiction that King Olaf had converted Greenland using Leif the Lucky as his evangelising agent had become accepted history. So the author of *Eirík's Saga* was faced with the problem of revising *Grænlendinga Saga* in the light of what he considered more reliable information. He had to discard Bjarni Herjólfsson altogether, in order to give to Leif the Lucky the glory of discovering Vínland on the eve of his mission to Greenland, as an earnest of God's approval. This fundamental change started a chain-reaction: details of Leif's voyage as recorded in *Grænlendinga Saga* then had to be distributed amongst later expeditions, starting with the voyage of his brother Thorstein.

The same zeal for historical accuracy, however misguided the results, explains the difference in the treatment of Guðríð. She had many notable descendants, including several bishops and prominent politicians, and it is not unlikely that the family retained traditions of her origins and childhood that the author of *Eirík's Saga* considered more accurate than her undignified arrival on the scene as a shipwrecked castaway in *Grænlendinga Saga*.

The two sagas are in more general accord over the account of the attempted colonisation of Vínland. They both agree that the leader of the colonising expedition was a wealthy Icelandic merchant called Thorfinn Karlsefni ('Makings of a Man'), who came to Greenland on a trading voyage around the year 1010. As was the custom, he spent the winter in the most eminent household in the area, Brattahlíð.

It so happened that Guðríð was also staying at Brattahlíð that winter. She had married Leif's brother, Thorstein Eiríksson, but Thorstein had died soon afterwards, leaving Guðríð a wealthy widow and owner of a farm at Lýsufjörd (Ameralikfjord) in the Western Settlement; this farm has been tentatively identified with the large manor of Sandnes, which was excavated in 1930.

'Guðríð was a woman of striking appearance; she was very intelligent and knew well how to conduct herself amongst strangers.' (*Grænlendinga Saga*).

'. . . very beautiful and a most exceptional woman in every respect.' (*Eirík's Saga*).

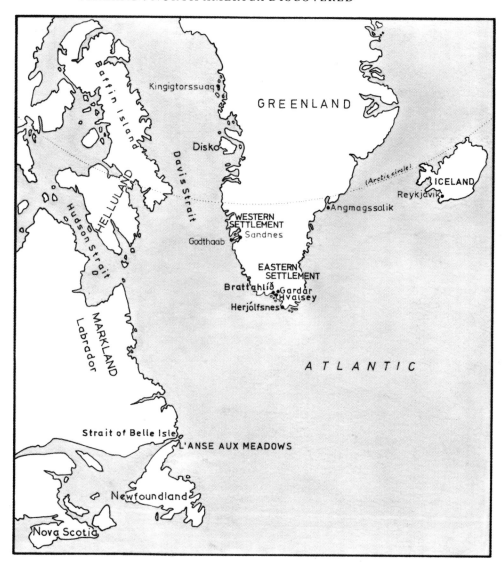

Viking discoveries to the west.

She was staying at Brattahlíð as one of the family, and Thorfinn Karlsefni soon fell in love with this attractive and eligible young widow. A marriage was arranged without difficulty, and no doubt the wedding ceremony took place in the tiny chapel that Thjóðhild had built 'not too close to the farmstead' at Brattahlíð.

That winter, too, there was much talk at Brattahlíð of going to Vínland. It seems clear that through Leif Eiríksson, the Brattahlíð family felt they had some sort of lien on Vínland; by building 'Leif's Houses', Leif the Lucky had become America's first real estate agent, and he was prepared to lease them to Thorfinn Karlsefni but not to sell them (*Grænlendinga Saga*). Even where no 'Leif's Houses'

132

were involved, as in *Eirík's Saga*, there could be considerable commercial value in founding a settlement in Vínland under the patriarchal aegis of Brattahlíð.

The expedition was mounted with great care and expense. The colonists took livestock of all kinds with them, for they intended a permanent settlement. There were sixty men and five women in the expedition, according to *Grænlendinga Saga*, but 160 people in three ships according to *Eirík's Saga*.

In both sagas, the expedition lasted for three years. Guðríð bore Thorfinn a son named Snorri, and this Snorri Thorfinnsson was the first recorded white child to be born in America. But the expedition was constantly menaced by the attentions of the native Indians, whom the Norsemen contemptuously called *Skrælings* (Wretches), the same name as the Greenlanders had already given to the native Eskimos. At first the two sides traded reasonably amicably, but it was not long before the Norsemen began to cheat the Indians, thus establishing an unhappy pattern for Europe's future relations with the natives of the New World. When the Indians returned, they came with hostile intent, and although the Norsemen managed to beat them off, it soon became clear to Thorfinn Karlsefni that they had not the reserves of manpower or arms to hold them off for long; although the iron weapons of the Norsemen were superior to those of the Stone Age Indians, they were not superior enough to be decisive in the long run. And so, after the third winter in Vínland, Thorfinn reluctantly abandoned his attempt to colonise the country, and returned to Greenland with a rich cargo of valuable produce.

He and his wife stayed on in Greenland for only a year or so, as guests at Brattahlíð. It may be presumed that they at least visited Guðríð's inherited farm at Lýsufjörd, if only to arrange its sale, and this has given rise to much romantic speculation about two archaeological finds made at the manor of Sandnes there: a lump of anthracite, and an arrow-head of quartzite. There are no deposits of anthracite in Greenland, and this lump has been associated with the kind of anthracite found in Rhode Island in New England. It was found in a deep layer in one of the rooms at Sandnes, and many have been tempted to see it as a souvenir brought back by the Karlsefni expedition. It now seems more likely, however, that it originated in Europe. The quartzite arrow-head is another matter, though. It was found in the north-west corner of the churchyard at Sandnes, and is undoubtedly of Indian origin, and the quartzite is identical with that of Labrador. It seems more than likely that this arrow-head

Quartzite arrow-head from Sandnes.

may have been a souvenir from one of the Norse sorties to Vínland.

From Greenland, Thorfinn Karlsefni and Guðríð returned to Iceland, and settled down on the family estate at Glaumbær in Skagafjörd, in the north; at Glaumbær today there is a well-preserved farmhouse made of turf and stone, dating from the eighteenth century, which now houses a local museum of traditional country life. *Grænlendinga Saga* also records a trading voyage to Norway, during which Thorfinn Karlsefni sold the produce he had collected in Vínland, including a carved gable-head made of maple-wood.

Guðríð survived her husband by several years. She went on a pilgrimage to Rome, and in her old age became a nun and lived at Glaumbær as an anchoress for the rest of her life. In her time she had travelled more widely than any other woman in the world—Norway, Iceland, Greenland, America, Rome; a remarkable feat by the farmer's wife who 'knew well how to conduct herself amongst strangers'.

In the autumn of 1965, neatly timed to appear exactly half-way between Leif Erickson Day and Columbus Day, Yale University in the United States published a bombshell: the so-called Vinland Map. It purported to be a medieval map of the world showing North America for the first time, round about the year 1440—a full fifty years before Columbus crossed the Atlantic. The scholars who published it called it 'the oldest map of the north Atlantic Ocean in existence', which 'records in graphic form the only documented pre-Columbian discovery of America'.

It was drawn on a sheet of parchment folded in two, measuring overall about ten inches by fifteen. The parchment was a light greyish-brown in colour, unusually translucent, which suggested that a good deal of the natural surface had been removed by scraping. The ink was reddish-brown and looked smudged, as if the Map had recently been subjected to extensive cleaning.

Most of the Map seemed to have been based on a World Map drawn by a Venetian cartographer called Andrea Bianco in 1436. What caused the sensation was the north-west corner of the Map, for it depicted a rather haphazard Iceland, a remarkably accurate Greenland, and a huge lumpy island labelled *Vinilanda* (or *Vimlanda*) *Insula*—Vínland. It had two large inlets on the east coast—possibly to represent the Hudson Strait and the Gulf of St Lawrence.

The argument advanced was that some scribe around the middle of the fifteenth century had married two maps to create a new one—

the Bianco map of 1436, and some hitherto unknown chart or charts made by the Norsemen in the thirteenth century perhaps, based on the Viking voyages to Vínland.

The Map was published in a volume called *The Vinland Map and the Tartar Relation*, and it aroused worldwide interest. No hint even of its existence had been allowed to leak out, even though the three scholars who edited the book had been working on it for seven years. At first it was hailed as the clinching proof that the Vikings really had discovered America, even though no further proof was really needed. But very soon doubts began to creep in, and scholars began to question whether the Map was as old as it was claimed to be, or even whether it was genuine.

Much of the early suspicion was aroused by the rather mysterious circumstances in which the Map had come to light. No one could, or would, say where it had come from, although it was revealed later that it had allegedly come from an unnamed private library in Europe, where it had lain for some sixty years, although no one could trace its history further back than that.

Originally, it seemed, the Map had been in a calf-bound volume which had contained two books written mostly on paper (not parchment, like the Map): these were a previously unknown account of a mission to the Mongols in 1245–47, called *The Tartar Relation*, and part of a thirteenth-century work called *Speculum Historiale* (*Mirror of History*). But these two books had become separated, and the calf-bound volume contained only the Vinland Map and *The Tartar Relation*.

The timetable of events connected with the appearance of the Map is of crucial importance:

In 1956, Professor Jón Jóhannesson published his clarification of the relationship between the two Vínland sagas, *Aldur Grænlendinga Sögu*, in a commemorative volume of essays entitled *Nordæla*. This was not published in English until six years later, but it immediately created great interest in the world of Norse scholarship.

In 1957, two works came separately onto the antiquarian book market in Geneva: the *Speculum Historiale* and *The Tartar Relation* with its accompanying Vinland Map. At the time, apparently, there was no reason to think the two works were connected. *The Tartar Relation* was a work of considerable interest in its own right, but it was the Vinland Map that was the focus of attention. Its dating depended entirely on the dating of *The Tartar Relation*, which was adjudged to be *c.* 1440 from the style of the handwriting and the

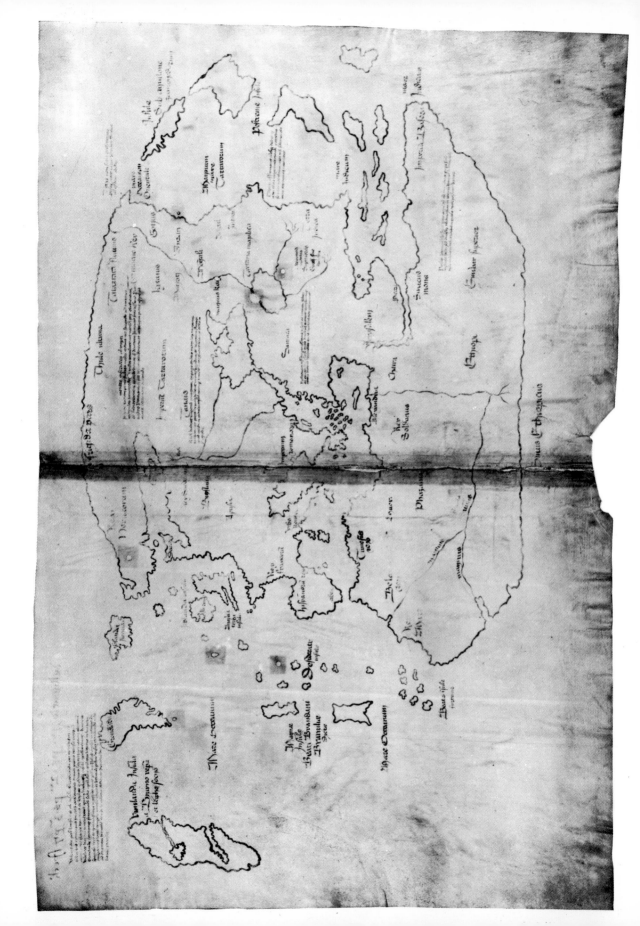

watermarks of the paper on which it was written. If the Vinland Map could be proved to have been associated with *The Tartar Relation* right from the start, then the Map, too, would be fifteenth century.

A London bookseller took the two works on spec, as it were. He offered the Vinland Map and *The Tartar Relation* to the British Museum. But the British Museum experts turned it down; there was not sufficient proof, they thought, that the Map and *The Tartar Relation* were directly associated, because although they both had worm-holes in them, the worm-holes did not match up exactly.

After its rejection by the British Museum, the London bookseller returned the Map and *The Tartar Relation* to Geneva, but bought the *Speculum Historiale* for his own list.

In Geneva, the Vinland Map and *The Tartar Relation* was bought by an antiquarian bookseller from New Haven in Connecticut called Lawrence Witten. The price he paid is reputed to have been $3,500. Mr Witten showed it to an expert at the Yale University Library— Thomas E. Marston, Curator of Medieval Literature; but Mr Marston, too, like the British Museum experts, was not convinced that the Map was sufficiently authenticated. Not only did the worm-holes not correspond, but one of the inscriptions on the Map referred to the *Speculum Historiale*, which was inexplicable at the time.

Then the long arm of coincidence came into play. Thomas Marston noticed the *Speculum Historiale* in the catalogue of the London bookseller early in 1958, and bought it as a routine acquisition for the Yale University Library. Now the New Haven bookseller, Lawrence Witten, came on the scene again: he pointed out that the *Speculum Historiale* and *The Tartar Relation* and the Vinland Map all seemed to match up—watermarks and handwriting. But in particular, the worm-holes could now be made to match up, if the *Speculum Historiale* was inserted between the Map and *The Tartar Relation*; the worms had gone off course as they browsed through the *Speculum Historiale*.

With that, the authenticity and date of the Vinland Map seemed to be assured. But after its publication in 1965, some searching questions began to be asked and some uncomfortable answers emerged. A Swedish scholar pointed out that the watermarks on the paper of the two books, far from being precisely datable to *c.* 1440, were common throughout Europe during the Middle Ages and the sixteenth century. Handwriting experts expressed doubts about the dating, too, and were unconvinced that the writing on the Map and the books was by the same hand.

The Vinland Map.

But the most damaging attacks on the Map came from expert cartographers, who doubted that such a map could ever have been made in the fifteenth century. In particular, it was Greenland that aroused their suspicions. Greenland is correctly shown as an island—yet it was not until the nineteenth century that northern Greenland was first explored and mapped. There is no evidence that the Norsemen ever went right round the island, and their northern hunting grounds never extended so far towards the Pole. The late Professor Eva Taylor of England made no pretence about her belief that Greenland had been copied from a modern map, and that the Vinland Map was therefore a forgery.

Only extensive chemical tests on the ink of the Map, to determine the spread of the ink through the parchment, could settle the argument; but such tests might also destroy the Map itself, and no results of any such tests have been announced.

While the cartographers wrangled, the attention of Norse scholars was focused on a Latin inscription that was scrawled in the top left-hand corner of the Map; because here, for the first time in an allegedly medieval document, the credit for discovering Vínland was given jointly to *two* men—Bjarni Herjólfsson and Leif the Lucky:

'By God's will, after a long voyage from the island of Greenland to the south, towards the most distant remaining parts of the Western Ocean sea, sailing southward amid the ice, the companions Bjarni and Leif Eiríksson discovered a new land, extremely fertile, and even having vines, the which island they named Vinilanda. . . .'

Bearing in mind the fact that the Vinland Map turned up in Geneva only a year after Professor Jón Jóhannesson had rehabilitated Bjarni Herjólfsson as the first discoverer of America, this Latin inscription has given rise to a delightfully scurrilous story in Iceland about its provenance: that the Vinland Map *is* modern, and was made in Iceland—not as a deliberate forgery, but as a joke.

The story goes that while Professor Jóhannesson was working on his researches into the Vínland sagas, he spent the winter at the home of a friend of his who was an artist and an enthusiastic amateur cartographer. They naturally discussed Bjarni and Leif the Lucky endlessly; and one idle evening, this artist scraped clean an old parchment map and embellished it with the kind of chart that the Norsemen might have made of Vínland had they been map-makers themselves, as a large serrated island. He simply made doodles for

Iceland and Greenland, ignoring the fact that the Norsemen could not have known that Greenland was an island. Then he added a crabbed Latin inscription in which he synthesised his friend's researches and solved the problem at a stroke—by awarding the palm of discovery jointly to Bjarni and Leif.

But now the plot thickens. For in a moment of hilarious inspiration, it is said that this 'Vínland Map' was despatched in jest to a certain royal personage in Scandinavia. But alas! The joke misfired. Somehow or other the Map fell into the hands of wicked and unscrupulous men, who with diabolical cunning gave it a spurious respectability through association with *The Tartar Relation*. The entire antiquarian book trade was duped, and through it the Yale University Library, which proceeded to publish, after vast academic toil, something that had started out merely as an idle amusement.

The story is only a joke, of course, the sort of academic joke that all Icelanders enjoy. At present it is impossible to make a definite assessment of the Vinland Map's authenticity except to say that it has still to be proved beyond any doubt to be genuine.

> The art of Biography
> Is different from Geography.
> Geography is about maps,
> Biography is about chaps.
> (Edmund Clerihew Bentley)

The two Vínland sagas are not geography. They are biography—stories about people who had engaged in a great adventure, perhaps the greatest adventure in the whole of the turbulent Viking Age. The saga-writers were concerned primarily with the way in which these people reacted to that adventure, and they have left us with a vivid portrait gallery of the men and women whose characters emerged under ordeal, the brave and the cowardly, the kind and the cruel, the noble and the infamous.

The accounts in the two sagas of the location and topography of Vínland cannot be reconciled. In *Grænlendinga Saga*, Thorfinn Karlsefni headed straight for 'Leif's Houses' in Vínland and stayed there for three years before abandoning the attempt to settle. In *Eirík's Saga*, on the other hand, he had to search for Vínland. He spent the first winter at a place called Straumfjörd, but the weather was so severe that he knew he had to go further south. He spent the second winter at a much more likely locality he called *Hóp* (Tidal Lake), where he found the wild wheat and wild grapes that spelt

Vínland—and also met his first Indians. After a pitched battle with them, he retreated back to Straumfjörd for his last winter in North America.

What all the early accounts of Vínland have in common is the fact of wild grapes, and wild wheat. As early as 1075, a bare sixty years after Thorfinn Karlsefni left Vínland, a German priest in Bremen called Adam completed a monumental history in Latin of the Archbishopric of Hamburg. His main informant about the geography of Scandinavia was the King of Denmark:

> 'He recounted that there was another island in that ocean which had been discovered by many and was called Wineland, because vines grow wild there and yield excellent wine, and, moreover, self-sown corn grows there in abundance; it is not from any fanciful imaginings that we have learned this, but from the reliable reports of the Danes.'

It was the fact of wild grapes that made Vínland so memorable to the Icelanders and Greenlanders and was reflected in its name. This provides a certain limit for the location of Vínland, for wild grapes have never grown farther north than Passamaquoddy Bay, between Maine and New Brunswick. Most scholars believe, on balance, that the Vínland of the sagas was an area as yet undefined somewhere in the region of New England. Some commentators have tried to broaden the possible area by suggesting that the first element in the name is not *vín* (wine) but *vin*, meaning 'meadowland', but this cannot be right: the two words could never have been confused in Icelandic, and the suggestion is a perversion of the explicit association of the name with wild grapes.

That is not to say, however, that there can be no Norse sites outside New England. The Vínland sagas are highly selective. It is quite probable that there were several expeditions to North America from Greenland or Iceland, to gather timber, for instance, or to hunt. There may even have been scattered settlements of fishermen or hunters, temporary or otherwise; for the Icelandic annals relate that round about 1120, a missionary bishop called Eirík Gnúpsson left Greenland on a mission to Vínland (this journey is also alluded to in the Latin inscription on the Vinland Map). The last documented reference to North America comes in the Icelandic annals for 1347, when a Greenland ship was storm-driven to Iceland after making a journey to Markland (Labrador), presumably to fetch timber or furs. Considering how relatively short and easy the journey was from Greenland to Labrador and Newfoundland and even farther south, it is unthinkable that the Greenlanders should not have exploited these resources in the centuries before the climate all over Europe worsened to such an extent that a Little Ice Age set in and made the northern seas too hazardous.

Countless books have been written, by scholars and amateurs alike, in an attempt to locate the Vínland of the sagas. The guesses have ranged all the way from Hudson Bay in the north to Virginia in the south. But no theory has found general acceptance, and every one has had to distort or disregard some of the available evidence.

The search for authentic archaeological evidence has been just as indefatigable, and for a long time just as fruitless. Perhaps the oldest of the Viking red-herrings is the Newport Tower in Rhode Island.

It stands in the middle of Touro Park, the municipal park of the old seafaring town of Newport. The town was founded in 1639, and the first documentary mention of the tower was made in 1677; but so curious a piece of architecture is it that many people have been tempted to believe that it was built by Vikings in pre-Columbian times. It is constructed of carefully mortared stones, it is cylindrical in shape and nine yards high. It has eight arches supported by round columns, with a number of windows and smaller apertures. Originally there was an upper storey, but the floor has collapsed, leaving only traces of a stair leading upwards. No one knows what the purpose of this tower was, whether it was a watch-tower or a windmill or even a church, but whatever its function it must surely have been built by English colonists in the seventeenth century. An American archaeologist, William S. Godfrey, excavated the ground around and inside the tower in 1948 and 1949, and all the finds he made there dated from colonial times; even so, enthusiasts still hanker for a pre-Columbian identification—though why the Vikings in the eleventh century rather than the English in the seventeenth should erect such a building is not a question anyone can answer.

The celebrated Kensington Stone is another Viking 'discovery' that has echoed down the years, ever since it was allegedly found embedded in the roots of a tree near the village of Kensington in western Minnesota in 1898. The farmer who found it, Olof Ohman, was a Swedish immigrant. The stone was dark-coloured and shaped like a slab measuring about thirty inches by sixteen by six, and weighing two hundred pounds. On one side there was an extremely long inscription in what purported to be runic lettering, as follows:

The Kensington Stone
with its alleged runic
inscription.

'. . . 8 Goths [Swedes] and 22 Norwegians on an expedition from
Vínland to the West. Our camp was by two skerries one day's
journey north from this stone. We went fishing one day. When we
came home found ten men red with blood and dead. AVM [Ave
Maria] deliver us from evil. Have ten men by the sea to look after
our ships 14 days' journey from this island. 1362.'

What gave the stone importance was that it should have been
found in the heart of the continent, with the suggestion that Scandinavians were penetrating so far inland from Vínland in the middle
of the fourteenth century. This is so implausible that the counter-
suggestion has been made that the stone was originally inscribed
somewhere near the coast, where it was found by Indians and carried
about by them as a cult object for hundreds of miles and several
generations.

But the main objection to the Kensington Stone is the runic
writing, which was promptly branded by scholars of the day as a

clumsy fraud, written in a mixture of Swedish, Norwegian and English. A few years later, however, it was bought by an enthusiast called Hjalmar R. Holand, who spent the rest of his life trying to prove its authenticity and weave a plausible story to account for the inscription. By his sheer insistence and energy he managed to create a lasting controversy and gain acceptance of the stone in some lay quarters; yet to this day, not a single archaeologist or linguist or runic specialist of any note believes that the Kensington Stone is anything other than a forgery, and a crude one at that. As one scholar has put it, 'It's like finding a telephone directory underneath a Viking ruin.'

In Canada, more than 3,000 miles away from Vínland, a gold-miner called James E. Dodd allegedly found a Viking grave on his claim near Lake Nipigon on the north shore of Lake Superior, Ontario. This was in 1930. It lay beneath a dyke of dark rock marked by a broad vertical vein of white quartz. The find, which is known as the Beardmore Find from the name of the nearby railroad station, is now in the Royal Ontario Museum of Archaeology in Toronto. It consisted of a broken iron sword, an axe-blade, a strip of bent metal that may have been part of a rattle, and some fragments which appear to be from the boss of a shield.

The find received no publicity for several years, but the museum authorities were able to identify the objects positively as being of eleventh-century Norse origin. Unfortunately, there had been no systematic excavation of the alleged grave, and in 1938 word went round that the objects had actually been brought to Canada from Norway some years previously by an educated young Norwegian called Lieutenant Johan Bloch, and that they had been seen in the basement of James Dodd's house. Strenuous efforts were made to disprove this allegation of 'planting' by the discoverer, but the mere breath of suspicion of a fraud or a hoax was sufficient to discredit the Beardmore Find, even though the objects were indisputably genuine. No one can now be sure of the truth of the matter, and so much doubt surrounds the circumstances of the finding that the objects themselves cannot be cited as archaeological proof of the presence of a Viking band in Ontario in the eleventh century.

In the last ten years, however, two areas of North America have attracted attention as possible Norse sites. Away in the north, in the Ungava Peninsula in the Province of Quebec, Canadian archaeologists have been studying a number of curious house-plans and structures that are claimed to have Norse features. Thomas E. Lee

The site of the largest building complex excavated by Helge Ingstad at L'Anse aux Meadows. The hollows were originally fireplaces and cooking-pits.

of the Centre d'Études Nordiques at Laval University has excavated a number of these sites. They include a large stone three-roomed building, several strange beacons on the shore, a 'great hall' on Pamick Island, and sunken stone-lined boxes not unlike the ember-pits of Viking farmhouses in Greenland and Iceland. Some of the habitation sites in the Ungava Peninsula can be identified as Eskimo or Indian, but others seem harder to explain. No European artefacts have been found in association with them, but Thomas Lee has suggested that they may have been Norse structures built by hunters near the migration lines of caribou herds. Who these Norsemen could have been is even more of a puzzle; and what were they doing there up in the wilds of the Canadian North? It is not impossible that they might have been survivors from the Western Settlement of Greenland, assuming that there were any survivors when it was abandoned in the middle of the fourteenth century; but unless more convincing evidence is found, the Ungava Peninsula sites cannot be considered seriously as Norse remains.

Much more significant, though, is the site at L'Anse aux Meadows in Newfoundland, where the Norwegian explorer Helge Ingstad claims to have found the site of 'Leif's Houses' in Vínland itself.

Épaves Bay lies ten minutes' walk to the west of the fishing village of L'Anse aux Meadows, on the north-eastern tip of Newfoundland. The sea is extremely shallow for a long way out, too shallow for even the smallest fishing boat to come in to land. The beach rises imperceptibly for a hundred yards or so until it reaches a marine terrace some thirteen feet high, which curves round in line with the head of the bay. The terrace consists mainly of sand and gravel covered by grass and heather. A little stream, Black Duck Brook, meanders through the meadowlands behind the terrace and cuts through it before it runs into the bay.

It is not a memorable area: not the sort of area to haunt the mind with dreams of milk and honey. No wild grapes grow there, no self-sown wheat, no rivers rich with succulent salmon. If this was Vínland, then Vínland was a confidence trick. The place has no outstanding natural resources, not even a natural harbour.

Yet here Helge Ingstad and his wife, Anne Stine Ingstad, excavated for seven seasons, and unearthed a complex of ruined buildings which can hardly be other than Norse.

There were eight of these structures in all, plus the remains of what seemed to be four or five boathouses separated by partition walls. The buildings had all been made with turf walls, and fell into three separate groups. The first group consisted of a four-roomed house that was eventually to provide the only spectacular find of the dig, a one-roomed building that may have been a cook-house, and a small, horseshoe-shaped structure without a hearth that could have been a roofed pen for sheep. The 'cook-house' was the first of the structures to be excavated in 1961, with the most encouraging results, for it contained a well-constructed hearth, a slate-lined cooking-pit full of coal and brittle-burned stones, and a stone-lined ember-pit full of charcoal—the kind of pit into which Norse house-wives swept the embers from the hearth at night to keep them alive until dawn.

The second group of buildings was even smaller: a three-roomed house of a type associated with Viking houses excavated in Thjórsárdale, in Iceland, and a small one-roomed building with a hearth that may have been used as a kitchen. In the house were found a burnt piece of bone needle, and a fragment of copper.

The third group was much the largest. It included a really large structure of six rooms, although they may originally have formed groups as separate houses. The walls were of turf, and there was evidence of post-holes to support the roof. Traces of a channel or groove near the walls may have been to slot in planks to provide interior panelling. The finds included a pebble lamp very like the Icelandic *kola*—a lump of stone with a depression on the top surface to hold the fish-oil that fuelled the wick.

It was at this house, right at the end of the 1964 season, that Anne

Anne Stine Ingstad uncovers a hearth in the first site to be excavated.

Stine Ingstad made a really dramatic discovery. All the rooms of the house had been cleared and measured and recorded. One room in particular, the room that faced south-east away from the sea and the wind, seemed to be associated with women's work, a sort of *dyngja* or bower. To round off the work, she dug a test trench just outside the door—and was rewarded with the appearance of a steatite spindle-whorl. It had been made from the bottom of a broken stone pot or bowl, for the bottom was concave and blackened by soot; but it was unmistakably Norse, and Helge Ingstad celebrated the find with an exultant article in the *National Geographic Magazine*: 'Vinland Ruins Prove Vikings Found the New World'.

But two years earlier there had come to light evidence which was just as convincing. In the 1962 season, Ingstad invited a number of Scandinavian archaeologists to take part in the excavations. A team from Iceland led by Dr Kristján Eldjárn was allotted the task of

146

excavating a curious round depression in the ground on the side of the marine terrace. What they found there turned out to be a smithy, with a broken stone anvil set into the earthen floor and hundreds of lumps of iron slag and a number of pieces of bog-iron ore, which is plentiful locally.

The extraction of iron from bog-iron was common practice in Iceland and Greenland at this time, and most large farms had their own smithy; but the process was quite unknown to the natives of North America. Radiocarbon tests on two of the pieces of charcoal found near the anvil yielded dates of AD 890 plus or minus ninety years, and AD 1060 plus or minus seventy years.

These dates accorded well with all the other radiocarbon dates taken from charcoal fragments or the turf walls of the other buildings. They all grouped themselves on either side of the AD 900 to 1000 period, and the overall effect is strongly indicative of occupation during the Norse period.

A striking feature of the excavation was the comparative paucity of artefacts found. However, against this should be set the negative evidence of the total lack of any artefacts from the colonial period in the sixteenth century, when Europeans were working from fishing stations in Newfoundland: no crockery, no glass, nothing to suggest colonial occupation was found on the site, and this seemed to refute those who believed that the site could not possibly be medieval.

Right at the end of the last season of digging in 1968 came a spectacular find that seemed to clinch the argument. The archaeologists returned to the main house in the first group, where they had merely made a trial excavation in 1961. In one of the rooms, right on the edge of a large cooking-pit, they found a ring-headed bronze pin. This was indisputably of Norse origin, probably from the middle of the tenth century.

A preliminary report on the excavations has recently been published by Anne Stine Ingstad, and it now seems to be beyond reasonable doubt that the site at L'Anse aux Meadows is Norse. It is difficult to say precisely how long the Norsemen occupied the site; there is no definite evidence that they had livestock with them, and the relatively small middens suggest that their stay was brief. It could also be that the three groups of houses represent the arrival of different Norse expeditions throughout the eleventh century.

Only one thing is absolutely certain: the site at L'Anse aux Meadows cannot be the Vínland of the sagas. Vínland, in the saga-writers' minds at least, lay far to the south, in the lands where the

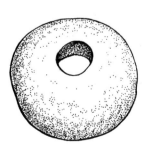

Steatite spindle-whorl from L'Anse aux Meadows.

wild grapes grew. These intriguing buildings in Newfoundland cannot possibly be the 'Leif's Houses' of *Grænlendinga Saga*. Rather, they are proof of the enduring seamanship and daring of the Vikings, who continued to visit the coasts of North America long after the pioneering voyages of Bjarni Herjólfsson, Leif the Lucky, and Thorfinn Karlsefni.

The epic surge of energy that sent the Vikings swarming westwards over the seas was finally exhausted on the shores of America. It came to nothing there, after all; but it has left the world an unforgettable legacy of heroism and adventure.

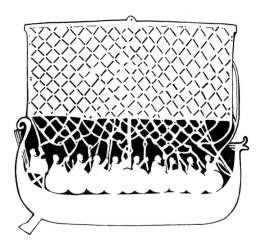

BOOKS FOR FURTHER READING

ALMGREN, B. (ed), The Vikings (C. A. Watts, London 1966)

ARBMAN, H., The Vikings (Thames & Hudson, London 1961)

BRØNSTED, J., The Vikings (Penguin Books, Harmondsworth 1965)

CORRÁIN, D. Ó, Ireland before the Normans (Gill & Macmillan, Dublin 1972)

FOOTE, P. G., and WILSON, D. M., The Viking Achievement (Sidgwick & Jackson, London 1970)

HAMILTON, J. R. C., Excavations at Jarlshof (HMSO, Edinburgh 1956)

INGSTAD, H., Westward to Vinland (Jonathan Cape, London 1969)

JONES, G. (transl), Egil's Saga (Syracuse University Press, USA 1960)

The Norse Atlantic Saga (Oxford University Press 1964)

A History of the Vikings (Oxford University Press 1968)

KENDRICK, T. D., A History of the Vikings (Methuen, London 1930)

KRISTJÁNSSON, J., Icelandic Sagas and Manuscripts (Saga Publishing Co., Reykjavík 1970)

KROGH, K. J., Viking Greenland (Copenhagen National Museum, 1967)

MAGNUSSON, M. and PÁLSSON, H., The Vinland Sagas (Penguin Classics, Harmondsworth 1965)

PAOR, M., and L. DE, Early Christian Ireland (Thames & Hudson, London 1958)

SAWYER, P. H., The Age of the Vikings (Edward Arnold, London, 2nd ed. 1971)

SIMPSON, J., Everyday Life in the Viking Age (Batsford, London 1967)

STENTON, F. M., Anglo-Saxon England (Oxford University Press, 1947)

TAYLOR, A. B., (transl), The Orkneyinga Saga (Oliver & Boyd, Edinburgh 1938)

WILSON, D. M., The Vikings and their Origins (Thames & Hudson, London 1970)

and KLINDT-JENSEN, O., Viking Art (Allen & Unwin, London 1966)

INDEX

150

ACKNOWLEDGMENTS

Thanks are due to the following for permission to reproduce black and white photographic material: Universitets Oldsaksamling, Oslo, pages 8 and 93; Statens Historiska Museum, Stockholm, pages 13 and 37; Controller of HMSO (Crown copyright), page 18; the Trustees of the British Museum, pages 24, 32, 33, 40; T. Haigh, page 28; National Museum of Denmark, Copenhagen, pages 30, 36, 66, 114, 115, 116, 119, 120, 121, 124, 133; Manuscript Institute of Iceland, pages 34 and 128; Guildhall Museum, London, page 38; University of Aberdeen Anthropological Museum, page 44; Dr Anna Ritchie, page 45 and, in association with the Department of the Environment, page 46; the Department of the Environment (Crown copyright), pages 48, 54 and 56; the National Museum of Antiquities of Scotland, page 52; the Manx Museum, Douglas, pages 59, 60 and 62; the National Museum of Ireland, Dublin, pages 67, 74, 76 and 77; Dr Breandán Ó Riordáin and the National Museum of Ireland, pages 68, 69, 70, 72 and 73; Tom Weir, page 79; Faroes National Museum, Torshavn, page 82; Viking Ship Museum, Roskilde, Denmark, page 90; National Museum of Iceland, Reykjavík, pages 91 and 104; Hörður Agustsson, page 97; Mats Wibe Lund Jr., Reykjavík, frontispiece and pages 88 and 105; Arnamagnean Institute, Copenhagen, page 99; Geisli Photographs, Reykjavík, pages 102 and 109; Iceland Tourist Bureau, page 117; Helge Ingstad, pages 126, 144 and 146; Smithsonian Institution, page 142; the Vinland Map on page 136 is reproduced by permission of the Yale University Press from *The Vinland Map and the Tartar Relation* by R. A. Skelton, Thomas E. Marston and George D. Painter. Copyright © 1965 by Yale University.

Thanks are due to the following for permission to reproduce coloured material: Universitets Oldsaksamling, Oslo, facing page 64; Viking Ship Museum, Roskilde, facing page 65; University of Aberdeen Anthropological Museum, facing page 80 (*top*); National Museum of Antiquities of Scotland, facing page 80 (*bottom*); National Museum of Ireland, facing page 81 (*top*); Geisli Photographs, Reykjavík, facing page 81 (*bottom*), facing page 96 (*bottom*), facing page 113 (*bottom*); Mats Wibe Lund Jr., Reykjavík, facing page 96 (*top*), facing page 113 (*top*); Gunnar Hannesson, facing page 97; Arnamagnean Institute, Copenhagen, facing page 112; the Royal Library, Copenhagen, jacket photograph.

The verse from *Egil's Saga* on page 10 is translated by Professor Gwyn Jones. The map on page 12 is based on one appearing in *A History of the Vikings* by the same author, published by the Oxford University Press. The drawing on page 51 is based on one by M. E. Weaver after A. Sorrell, and those on pages 71 and 75 on photographs supplied by Dr Breandán Ó Riordáin.